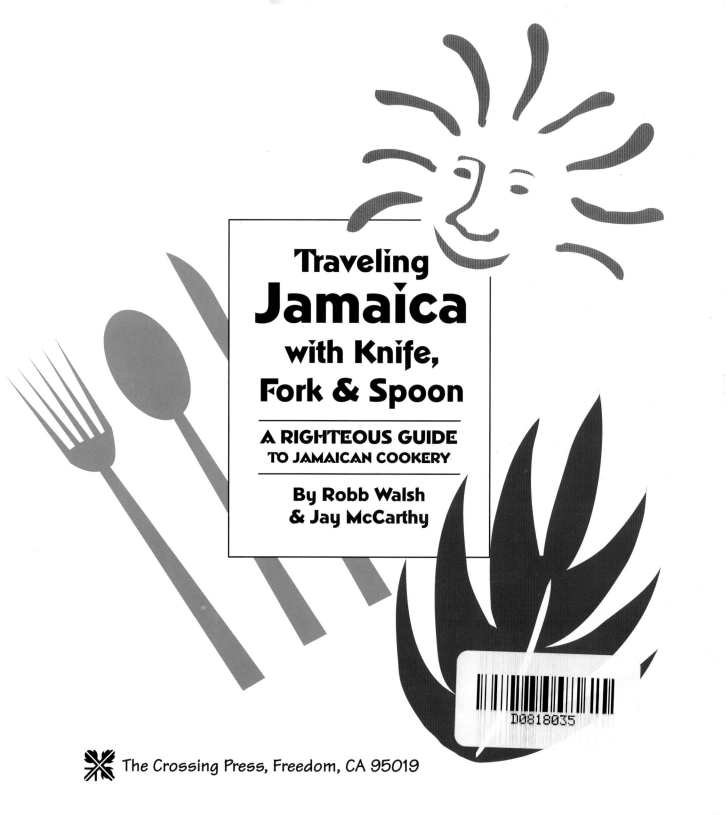

Traveling
Jamaica
with Knife,
Fork & Spoon

A RIGHTEOUS GUIDE
TO JAMAICAN COOKERY

By Robb Walsh
& Jay McCarthy

The Crossing Press, Freedom, CA 95019

Dedication

This book is dedicated with love to Katie, Julia, Caswell and Brenn.

Acknowledgments

The authors wish to thank all the Jamaicans who gave us their time, their recipes and their advice. We especially thank Sister Fire for sharing her cooking talents and the gentle philosophy of the Rastafarians with us. We are grateful to Sandra Forrester for inviting us into her home and showing us her family recipes.

And thanks to Boris Reid at the Native Restaurant in Montego Bay for the hot sauce, Berty Jones in the Black River Market for the peanut tonic, Joyce Sampson of Table Talk Restaurant in Port Antonio for the help, Urnal "Spirit" Taylor for the spices in Boston Beach, Norman Grant and Keble Munn for the tour of the Mavis Bank Coffee Plant, Dr. Barnaby for his stinking toe stories, Alex Twyman for a great cup of coffee, Tete Mendez for the fried fish, Joy Manson for the bammies, Mr. Ashman for the ackee, Arthur Alexander and Cherry Baker for the curry goat on Spur Tree Hill, Myrna Bryan for the mannish water and Lovena Braham for the pompano.

We also thank Grand Lido, Hedonism, Half Moon Golf, Tennis and Beach Club, Round Hill, Sandals, Tryall Golf, Tennis and Beach Club, Devon House, Temple Hall and the Trident Hotel for all the recipes and the great rum drinks.

Special thanks to Jay McCarthy's family in Jamaica, especially Gloria Palomino, Ralph and Hilda James, and Sheila and Michael James for all their help and hospitality and a very special thanks to Jay's sister, Valery Parchment, our guide and protector.

For their help and support, we thank Juli McCarthy and Cindy Goldman. Thanks also to Marion Winik for the great writing tips, to Dennis Hayes for the encouragement and to Dave DeWitt for recommending us to write this book in the first place.

Library of Congress Cataloging-in-Publication Data

Walsh, Robb.
      Traveling Jamaica with knife, fork & spoon : a righteous guide to Jamaican cookery /
by Robb Walsh & Jay McCarthy.
                          p. cm.
      Includes index.
      ISBN 0-89594-698-X (pbk.)
      1. Cookery, Jamaican. 2. Restaurants—Jamaica—Guidebooks. 3. Jamaica—
Guidebooks. I. McCarthy, Jay. II. Title.
      TX716. J27W35 1995
      641.597292—dc20   94-24445
                                                                        CIP

Contents

Introduction

A Righteous Taste of Jamaica

In the fall of 1993, Jay McCarthy and I squeezed into a small Japanese rental car with his beautiful sister, Valery Parchment, and set off on a Jamaican food odyssey. For two weeks, we rumbled down dirt roads, through tropical jungles, over mountain passes and into strange little backwaters looking for the definitive versions of Jamaica's most famous dishes. We took along a camera, a tape recorder, a couple of very hearty appetites and our den mother, Valery.

Valery Parchment has lived in Jamaica for most of her life. She did most of the driving and made sure that the locals didn't give us the tourist treatment—Valery is a tough cookie and fluent in Jamaican patois. We were very thankful she was there to save us when an angry crowd gathered at the Port Antonio market to accuse us of being CIA operatives. (The camera and tape recorder seemed like spy tools.) Her translations of roadside recipes were also indispensable. And on more than one occasion, she got to play designated driver when we sampled too many local libations.

In retrospect, it seems like a ridiculously ambitious idea to try to eat your way across the entire island of Jamaica in two weeks. But we were full of enthusiasm and also big enough eaters to endure four and five meals a day when duty demanded.

Our mission was to gather the authentic recipes from each of Jamaica's very different regions. In the wet and jungly northeast, we sampled Rastafarian vegetarian cooking. In Boston Beach, we tried the jerk pork. In the skyscraping peaks of the Blue Mountains, we sipped the world's finest coffee. In the drier south near Mandeville, we ate goat dishes, like curry goat and mannish water (a delicious goat soup). In Faiths Pen we ate cow cod soup and drank herbal tonics guaranteed to cure a wide variety of ailments. And finally in Negril, Montego Bay, and Ocho Rios, I sampled the cooking (and bartending) at some of the most famous resorts in the world.

From the lush jungles of the north to the desert flatlands of the Cockpit country, we discovered that Jamaica has an incredible variety of climates and agricultural specialties. Within each region we found different ingredients, different subcultures, and different food traditions.

We also learned from our research that, throughout Jamaica's history, each newly arrived ethnic group has added another layer of complexity to Jamaican cuisine. Spanish, French, British, and East Indian dishes are all part of Jamaican cooking. And the Amerindians who settled Jamaica long before Columbus came to the New World made some of the largest contributions of all.

The native Arawak Indians cooked meat on a wooden grate called a *barbacoa*—a tradition that continues today in the form of Jamaica's famous jerk barbecue. The Arawaks grew cassava, hot peppers, corn, sweet potatoes, callaloo, beans, pineapples, and papaya, all of which are still staples of Jamaican cooking. The cassava pancakes called "bammies" and the rich stew know as pepperpot are two Arawak Indian dishes that have survived virtually unchanged.

The Spanish brought goats, cattle, and pigs to Jamaica along with many of their own food traditions. Fried food was introduced to Jamaica by the Spanish, and so were bananas, plantains, citrus fruits, ginger, and coconut. Escoveitch fish, pea soup, rice and peas, and paella are all popular Jamaican dishes of Spanish origin.

African slaves, imported to work in the sugarcane fields, cultivated their own okra, yams, and callaloo. From their homelands, they brought such dishes as the tamale-like package of sweetened starch called a dokano.

The English brought to Jamaica ackee, breadfruit, mango, and black pepper from the South Pacific, along with imported salted and pickled foods. Roast beef, puddings, and the habit of calling every nonalcoholic drink "tea" are part of the British food heritage of Jamaica. Under British rule, slave owners were required to provide slaves with a certain amount of salted fish each year. Saltfish and ackee, often called the Jamaican national dish, traces its origins to this slave wage.

Fleeing the slave revolt in Haiti, French refugees to Jamaica brought a variety of cooking traditions to the island. The pickled-herring spread called Solomon Gundy is a corruption of the old French word for an elaborate salad called a *salmagundy*. The patty, Kingston's most popular lunch, is derived from the French *pâté*.

After the abolition of slavery in the 1830s, workers from India and China were brought to Jamaica. Indian workers introduced the many curry recipes that are popular in Jamaica, most notably curry goat.

Unified by common ingredients—such as fish, tropical fruits and the thyme and allspice that grow all over the island—Jamaican cooks share many of the same recipes throughout the country. But separations between classes, ethnic groups, and regions have kept alive many fascinating distinctions.

Although you can find produce from all over Jamaica in any of the island's local markets, regional preferences still dominate. Just take a bite of each region's own version of dokono. In the south, around Mandeville, the banana leaves are usually stuffed with a cassava mixture, because cassava is the area's dominant starch. In Montego Bay and the northwest, where corn is grown, cooks use cornmeal; in Port Antonio and the northeast, they most often use green bananas.

Cooks in each region are quite content to borrow freely from their neighbors; you can eat curry goat or jerk pork anywhere on the island. At the same time, each region is extremely proud of its own special dishes. Everyone knows that the original jerk pork can be found only in Boston Beach, and that for the definitive goat curry you have to visit the little restaurants of Spur Tree Hill outside Mandeville. The best roasted breadfruit is in Port Antonio, and the finest patties are in Kingston.

To write a cookbook that really gets to the heart of Jamaican food—a righteous Jamaican cookbook—we went to the source of each traditional Jamaican dish. In the process, we collected not just recipes, but also a series of impressions of the colorful places and people that give Jamaican food its spicy character. We hope you enjoy reading and cooking from this book as much as we enjoyed our research for it.

—Robb Walsh

Tryall Golf, Tennis & Beach Club

MONTEGO BAY

Sandals Royal Caribbean

Half Moon Bay Resort

Jamaican Fast Food

OCHO RIOS

Town Talk Restaurant

Sandra Forester's House, Titchfield

Fairy Hill Beach, Sister Fire's "Garden of Eating"

PORT ANTONIO

Boston Beach

Jerk Paradise

Faiths Pen

Negril

Middle Quarters

MANDEVILLE

Old Harbour

KINGSTON

Hardwar Gap, "The Gap" Restaurant

Grand Lido Resort

YS Falls Papaya Plantation

BLACK RIVER

Blue Mountain coffee at Alex Twyman's

Mavis Bank coffee pulperies

Pepper Shrimp Ladies

The best Mannish Water we ever had

Pickapeppa Factory

Devon House, Temple Hall, The Fish Place

Peanut Wine at Berty Jones' stand

Curry Goat Stands

Ashman's Ackee Factory

Fish Ladies and The Bammy Queen

Robb, Jay and their map

Chapter 1

From Fairy Hill to World's End

A Jamaican Food Odyssey

Downtown Port Antonio

Narrow shafts of intense morning sunlight slant in through chinks in the wooden walls of the dark kitchen. Clouds of smoke curl through the sunbeams. The only other light comes from an open wood fire under a pot of furiously boiling red peas.

The steamy aroma of the peas blends with the smell of wood smoke and vegetables. An old black man with white hair which stands straight up from the top of his head is cutting up chickens. His knife resembles a machete. At his feet, five cats with twitching tails sit waiting for a handout.

The counter tops are covered with the produce bought at the market this morning. In the strange light, they make an exotic still life—cho-cho squash, green bananas, breadfruit and huge yams nesting in a bale of the Jamaican greens called callaloo.

The kitchen of Town Talk restaurant in downtown Port Antonio doesn't look like any restaurant kitchen Jay or I have ever seen before. We came looking for breakfast, but Joyce Samson, the owner, apologizes that the restaurant doesn't open until lunch time. She invites us to look around anyway.

Chef Jay McCarthy and I have set out on a mission. Over the next two weeks, we will visit every region of Jamaica, eating at roadside stands, visiting restaurants, interviewing cooks, collecting recipes and attempting to understand the whole subject of Jamaican cuisine.

But before we visit the fancy restaurants of Kingston and the posh resorts of Ocho Rios and Montego Bay, we have decided to start at the beginning—with the food of the people. We make a strange sight in the local food markets and hole-in-the-wall restaurants—two out-of-towners with cameras, tape recorders, and notebooks asking questions about bananas and cooking herbs. But with the help of Jay's sister, Valery Parchment, a lifelong resident of the island, we eventually convince most of the people we talk with that we aren't spies or tourists, but students of Jamaican cooking.

Our designated driver, Valery Parchment

Jay spent the better part of his childhood in Jamaica, so he is already well versed in the crazy language of Jamaican food. He already knows recipes for mannish water, stamp and go, rundown, fish tea, Solomon Gundy, and dokono. As a professional chef, Jay is also quick to pick up on the cooking techniques and guess the ingredients of the food we eat. And he is always at home in a kitchen.

We chatted with Joyce Samson for a while about her restaurant before we left. Town Talk restaurant is famous in these parts for its "I-tal food." No, the word isn't short for *I-talian*; I-tal is the cooking style of the Rastafarians.

The Rastafarians are gentle people with a very spiritual approach to life. They are the people who introduced the world to reggae, dreadlocks, and the sacramental smoking of marijuana, or ganja, as it's known here. The Rastafarians' ideas are the dominant strain in contemporary Jamaican culture. Their philosophy about food is remarkably similar to that of the vegetarian movement in the United States, and their I-tal cooking style has been responsible for bringing new respect to traditional Jamaican dishes, once looked down on because they originated in the days of slavery.

Jay and I discuss I-tal cooking over breakfast at another strange little restaurant in downtown Port Antonio, this one called China Garden. While we sip mint tea with whole clumps of mint stalk floating in it, a man at the next table overhears our conversation and introduces himself.

He is barefoot and he sports a huge mane of dreadlocks under his cap. Ragamuffin is his Rasta name, he tells us. We ask him to explain what I-tal food is. "It's not just food: I-tal is the Rasta way of life," Ragamuffin says. "It means no shoes, no fancy clothes, food without meat or salt—a simpler way of life."

Ragamuffin's breakfast consists of boiled green bananas, callaloo, and a breadfruit dumpling. "Is that I-tal food you're eating?" we ask him. Ragamuffin explains that while this is not an I-tal restaurant, his vegetarian breakfast is consistent with the I-tal philosophy of eating. But he explains that what is and isn't I-tal depends on whom you talk to. Some say that chicken is OK, others disagree.

But every Rastafarian agrees that pork, red meat, and salt are not part of the I-tal diet, and that vegetables, fruits, and fish are. If we want to eat the finest I-tal food prepared by someone who truly understands the I-tal philosophy, we are told, we should go to Fairy Hill Beach and look for a Rasta woman named Sister Fire.

Before we leave, we scout around the charming city of Port Antonio. There are few tourists here, but there's also very little of the hustle and grime of big city life that one finds in Kingston. Along the waterfront we see a boy walking down the street carrying a huge freshly caught fish by the tail. It's a silk, Jay tells me, a large snapper that is exceptionally flavorful.

Port Antonio seems wonderfully rural and colorfully tropical. It is a city that was built on the banana trade. The banana wharf made famous by the Harry Belafonte song "Day-O" is here. "Come, Mister Tallyman, tally me bananas," we sing as we drive by. But the banana trade is no longer very active in Port Antonio. Legend has it that in the heyday of the banana business, around the turn of the century, Port Antonio also became the birthplace of the Jamaican tourist industry.

It was the enterprising banana moguls who first brought Americans to Jamaica. The boats were loaded with green bananas, which ripened on the way to the eastern coast of the United States. After the

Blue Lagoon

boats were unloaded, they sailed back to Jamaica empty. Before long, according to the stories, the idea of filling the empty banana boats with tourists caught on. But although I've read this account in many tour guides and books about Jamaica, I have never figured out how all those tourists got home again.

It's something to wonder about as we drive east out of Port Antonio, heading for the spectacular scenery of the coast road. We pull the car over again and again to gawk at the impossibly perfect views like palm-studded Monkey Island sitting in a little turquoise cove, and the deep violet water of the famous Blue Lagoon. This is certainly the most beautiful drive in Jamaica, if not the world.

Fairy Hill Beach

It takes twenty minutes to negotiate the rutted final half mile of dirt road in our little rented car. But when Jay, Valery, and I finally arrive at Fairy Hill Beach, we realize we have discovered Jamaica as it used to be—an unspoiled and undeveloped tropical paradise.

Before us, a perfect white crescent beach is framed by gigantic sea grape trees. Rounded gray cliffs that look like elephant's legs rise beyond the beach and parade off to the horizon on either side of the cove.

As we admire the scene, a smiling black man and his son ride their chestnut horses bareback through the gentle waves. The water is striped in turquoise, dark blue, and bright green. Just off the shore, a black man with dreadlocks is fishing from a bright red dugout canoe.

The only commercial ventures on the beach are tiny stands selling beer, cigarettes, sunscreen, and snacks, and a tiny open-air kitchen. After putting on our bathing suits and taking a dip, we explore the jungle bordering the beach. We munch on the sweet and sour sea grapes we find hanging from the trees, and look for other wild tropical fruits.

Poking through the bushes, Jay and I come across a couple of crustaceans he identifies as land crabs. Land crabs are a little bigger than blue crabs, and they are a great delicacy, he says. They are called land crabs since they live in holes in the ground rather than underwater. We catch two by stepping on their backs, and carry them squirming and snapping to the open-air restaurant.

The proprietor of this one-picnic table eatery is a middle-aged black man named Morris who is happy to boil up our crabs with some Scotch bonnet peppers we bought that morning in the Port Antonio market (see his recipe on page 87).

Scotch bonnets are among the hottest peppers in the world. Thin-skinned, they are sometimes picked green, but they are more often seen in markets in their ripe yellow-orange or red form. They are related to the Mexican habanero pepper. Due to their extreme potency, they must be used with extreme caution, and are often simply thrown into the pot with the food to be fla-vored and then removed and discarded, the method used by Morris in making our pepper crabs.

As we wash down our crabs with a couple of cold Red Stripe beers at Morris's picnic table, we ask him if he knows a woman named Sister Fire. "That's Sister Fire," Morris says, pointing. She is sitting on a rock by the freshwater spring about fifty yards away.

Sister Fire is washing her hair. A few minutes later she comes over to our table and we introduce ourselves. She is a very beautiful woman with bright green eyes. She tells us that she recently returned to Jamaica after running a restaurant in Fort Lauderdale, Florida, for many years. To our delight we find that she speaks American English, so we have no problem communicating. "They call me Sister Fire because I use a lot of peppers in my cooking," she tells us with a smile as she dries her dreadlocks.

On the hill above the beach Sister Fire runs an open-air restaurant, where, she agrees, she will prepare us a lunch of "I-tal food." We make our way back up the rutted road and find Sister Fire's restaurant in a clearing by the side of the road.

The restaurant consists of her combined dwelling and kitchen and a couple of picnic tables. Sister Fire sits us down at a picnic table with a glass of freshly made guava juice (see the recipe on page 69).

Our first course is a plate of sautéed ripe plantains. They are so sweet and gooey inside that they taste almost like candy; their outsides are crispy and caramel-colored. As we savor them, Sister Fire stirs up a vegetable rundown, a vegetarian stew made with cho-cho squash, potatoes, carrots, and onion, simmered in coconut milk with Scotch bonnet peppers and native herbs (see the recipe on page 167). The aromas of ginger, allspice, and fresh thyme envelop us, and before long our mouths are watering.

While she cooks, Sister Fire explains that her combined kitchen and dwelling is built Rasta-style, without any nails or metal fasteners. Each piece of wood is fitted and fixed in place with wooden pegs. The view of the beach from her open-air kitchen is a spiritual experience in itself.

In a tree outside, we see some bananas, going black with age, hanging from a limb. Sister Fire notices our interest, and explains that she hangs her leftover fruit from the trees for the bats and birds to eat. This is not only a St. Francis-style act of kindness; it also keeps the

What does I-tal Mean?

The letter "I" is very special in the language of the Rastafarians, who also call themselves the Rasta-Far-I. The lone capital "I," signifying a divine sense of self, appears in many Rasta word constructions. *Divine becomes I-vine; Ethiopian becomes I-thiopian. Acording to Sister Fire, I-tal is the Rastafarian version of the word vital.* Hence, the Rastas seek to lead the I-tal, or vital, way of life through, among other things, vital, or I-tal, food.

birds and bats from eating so much of the good fruit.

The stew is outstanding: The coconut milk has reduced to a thick, spicy sauce, and the vegetables are perfectly cooked. Sister Fire sits down to join us, and we ask her to contribute a few recipes, which she does.

After she outlines the recipes, Sister Fire explains the gentle philosophy of the Rastafarians, which reminds us of the utopian thinking of the Woodstock era. All around us, guava trees, banana trees, and papaya trees lean under the heavy burden of their fruits. The garden of Eden comes to mind, probably because Sister Fire calls this place "Peppers Garden-of-Eating Restaurant." It is a business without electricity, a cash register, walls, or a roof. It's not a restaurant—it's a Rasta-rant.

Sister Fire, cooking at her Rasta-rant

Titchfield

"Nobody won dead fe' hungry in Jamaica," laughs Sandra Forrester as she shows us around her yard. Nobody dies of hunger in Jamaica.

Sandra is referring to the incredible plenty that hangs from the trees and grows in the little gardens all over Jamaica. On her tiny plot of land, Sandra grows bananas, coffee, mangoes, yams, sugarcane, and several fruits I've never seen before—jumbline, a pale green star-shaped fruit; othaiti apples, said to be introduced to Jamaica from Tahiti by Captain Bligh; the starchy, tuber-like breadfruit, and the strange Jamaican staple called ackee.

We met Sandra Forrester the night before at the Bonnie View Hotel. The restaurant sits on top of a steep mountainside. From the deck, you get a heart-quickening view of Port Antonio's harbor, so directly below you that it seems like you're hovering over the city in a helicopter.

Robb, Sandra and Jay

We had just eaten the Bonnie View's version of escoveitch fish (see the recipe on page 136). The fried fish is served in a tart and spicy sauce of vinegar, onions, peppers, squash, and allspice. The name is derived from the Spanish *escabeche*, which means pickled. We asked our waiter if we could meet the chef to ask for her recipe. Reluctantly, the shy and soft-spoken Sandra Forrester appeared from the kitchen, wiping her hands on her apron.

Sandra, it turns out, leads a busy life. She cooks nights at the Bonnie View, but every morning she rises early to bake the colorful coconut cookies called gizzada (see the recipe on page 200) that her friends sell for her on the streets. We wangled an invitation to watch her do her baking at her home this morning.

At 8:30 in the morning, Sandra's house is bustling with activity.

The smell of baking cookies and toasted coconut fills the air. Sandra is rolling out dough on the kitchen counter. Her rolling pin is an empty rum bottle. She cuts the dough into rounds with a plastic cup, and expertly crimps the edges in a wavy pattern. Then she carefully fills the shells with colored shredded coconut flavored with ginger.

Jay asks to try his hand at making gizzadas, and soon the room fills with laughter as we admire his slightly misshapen first attempts. But he soon gets the hang of it and helps Sandra turn out one hundred gizzadas, as she does every morning. We sample a few hot out of the oven.

Then Sandra shyly offers us an unexpected treasure. She takes down from the living-room bookshelf a handwritten cookbook containing a collection of her family's favorite recipes. We eagerly scan the pages and jot down her recipes for the sweet bread called bulla, for vegetable dishes like red pea soup and rice and peas, and other old Jamaican classics.

You might expect some resentment from a woman who works as hard for as little money as Sandra does. But in fact she is one of the most cheerful, kind-hearted people we have ever met. As we drive away, Sandra waves good-bye from the front porch of her modest frame house. The friendship she has shown to three strangers, bringing them into her home and sharing her skills and her family's cooking heritage, will never be forgotten.

Boston Beach

On our way to Boston Beach, we pull the car over near a huge pimento tree that grows wild by the side of the road. "This is the secret of great jerk," says Jay.

Although the pimento tree's tiny berries, known as allspice, are familiar to cooks the world over, here in Jamaica, Jay explains, the leaves and wood of the tree are also used in cooking and for many other purposes. He crushes a leaf and holds it to my nose to give me a sample of the intense aroma. Then he proceeds to take off his shoes and stuff a couple of leaves into them. "Pimento leaves are great sneaker deodorizers," he explains.

The scent of burning pimento wood greets us as we cross the bridge. We park the car by the road and enter into the smoky little hamlet of Boston Beach, the jerk center of the universe. It's not a town, really, but just a collection of "jerk shacks," bars, and spice stores.

The jerk men tout their respective specialties as we approach. "Check this out, mon," says one, holding out a link of jerk sausage. They all aggressively peddle their own special blends of wet jerk seasoning and swear they've got the freshest meat.

What sets Boston Beach jerk apart from the jerk barbecue found all over the island of Jamaica is the pimento wood it is cooked over. Pimento is plentiful in the rain forests of northeast Jamaica.

In two visits to Boston Beach, we discover that Jamaican jerk is much the same as the barbecue in our home state of Texas in at least one respect—timing is important. Lunch at 2:30 was disappointing because the meat, which had been cooking since the morning, was overly dry. A repeat visit the next day a little before noon was much more satisfying.

"I should have known better," I say. "At Louis Mueller's barbecue in Taylor, Texas, you have to get there before 11 a.m. if you hope to get any ribs." It's obviously the same story in Boston Beach. The cooking is timed so the meat is perfectly done for the lunch rush around noon; dropping by in the midafternoon is a mistake. The fried cornbread sticks, called festival, and the roasted breadfruit are also much better at 11:30 a.m.

Like Texas barbecue, jerk is served on a sheet of butcher paper and eaten with your hands. There's plenty of beer and soda available, and the starchy breadfruit and festival will fill you up quickly. The jerk pork is our favorite, and we are fascinated by the coarse sausage. But the most interesting exercise in Boston Beach is trying to figure out the recipe for the famous wet jerk rub. We buy several bottles and stick our fingers in them to try to deduce the ingredients. This is an eye-opening exercise at 11:30 in the morning, since jerk rub contains a lot of scotch bonnet peppers. The rub is incredibly hot in its raw form, but after cooking for awhile it tones down to a pleasant spicy burn. Later, after several experiments, we hit on a version of Boston Beach wet jerk rub that tastes very close to the original. (See the jerk barbecue recipes on pages 114-141.)

What can we say?

Wandering around Boston Beach, we also spend some time talking with Urnal ("Spirit") Taylor, who runs a very colorful spice store there. The name of his business, which takes up nearly the entire front of the store, is: Spirit Farmer's Production Pepper and Spice and Spices Garden Number One.

Strewn on the floor and makeshift shelves is a vast array of straight-from-the-jungle herbs and spices, which we ask Urnal to identify. We buy some fresh allspice berries and rough cinnamon bark. The outer bark of the cinnamon tree is not as delicate in flavor or as fragrant as the inner bark shavings, which are sold as cinnamon sticks. But although the outer bark doesn't have as strong a cinnamon aroma, it does have an intense cinnamon burn. We wonder if this outer bark might not be the secret of hot cinnamon candies, and we also wonder how it might taste in wet jerk rub.

World's End

Driving up the main road to the Blue Mountain coffee region, we pull over for a rest and discover we have stopped in front of the famous Sangster's Distillery. Dr. Ian Sangster, an immigrant from Scotland, started this remarkable little operation on the side of a cliff in 1973. Since then he has been producing some of Jamaica's best rums, but he is especially famous for his tropical fruit liqueurs.

We ask if we can look around, and before long we are joined by a hostess who asks us if we would like to sample the Sangster's line. Although it is not yet eleven in the morning, we reluctantly agree to taste a liqueur or two since we probably won't be by here again when the place is open.

Sangster's makes rum and Jamaica's tastiest liqueurs

But our hostess will have none of our squeamishness. She begins to open bottle after bottle of liqueur, handing us shot glasses of each. "It's just a tiny little taste," she says dismissing our protests. Before long we have sampled orange, banana, and ortanique liqueurs, aged rums, and a staggering number of liquors we can't even keep track of.

We buy a couple of bottles of our favorites in the gift shop, and get a booklet with some of Sangster's drink recipes before we get back in the car. Luckily, Valery, who is driving, was wise enough not to do any tasting. But Jay and I are definitely ready to sample some coffee.

Mavis Bank

As we climb above four thousand feet, the misty blue peaks of the mountains are obscured by a jungle of flowering bushes that begin to close in on the asphalt. Our four-wheel-drive vehicle burrows through the foliage, leaving a shower of white flower petals in the air behind us.

Finally, we reach the top of Jamaica's Blue Mountains. From the lookout, it seems as if you could drop a rock off the cliff and hit downtown Kingston. It has taken an hour and a half to drive 25 miles. Now we have only a short drive around the mountain to Mavis Bank, one of the most famous Blue Mountain coffee pulperies. It's a long way to go for a cup of coffee.

But Jamaican Blue Mountain coffee is worth going out of your way for. It sells in New York for up to thirty-five dollars a pound. In Tokyo it sells for sixty dollars a pound, or ten dollars a cup. It's by far the most expensive coffee in the world.

The Mavis Bank Central Factory is one of four pulperies which together process all Blue Mountain coffee. These plants may not accept coffee from any grower outside the official Blue Mountain area, and Blue Mountain growers can sell their coffee nowhere else. This arrangement began after World War II, when the Jamaican Coffee Board was established to insure the quality of Blue Mountain coffee.

Norman Grant, the head of operations at Mavis Bank, takes us on a tour of the facility. He explains the process by which the "cherry berries," as the raw coffee fruits are known, are turned into green beans ready for roasting.

After removing the outer "cherry," a fruit-like coating, the beans are fermented to remove the mucilage that clings to the bean. Then the beans are washed in water and spread out on the "barbecue," a huge patio where the beans dry in the sun. They are turned every 30 to 40 minutes, then covered overnight. The beans remain on the barbecue for three days.

Next, a hulling machine removes the bean's paper-like covering, called parchment, and the green beans are polished and graded. The graded beans are then hand-sorted to remove discolored and broken beans.

But the highlight of the process for us is a cup tasting. Quality control in the coffee business is not a scientific or mechanized process. Samples from each batch of coffee are roasted, ground, and put into a cup with boiling water. Then a trained coffee taster starts slurping.

Actually, "slurping" is putting it mildly. As Norman Grant spins the rotating table with our seven coffee samples, he uses a spoon to move the floating grounds out of the way,

Robb, picking coffee beans in the Blue Mountains

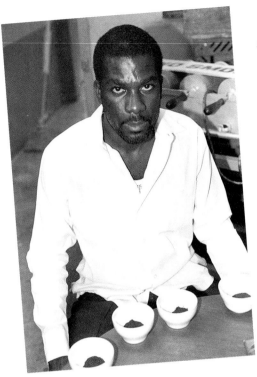

Norman Grant prepares to slurp

and, after assessing the bouquet from a cup, he sucks back a mouthful of coffee with more force than seems humanly possible. This intense, whistling intake of breath is intended to coat the back of the throat with a fine spray of coffee, Grant explains.

We give it a try, and both of us started coughing. After a few more attempts, we get the hang of it, though we never work up to the frenzy of Grant's slurp. The seven samples we try illustrate the wide range of quality in Blue Mountain coffee.

The first is very good; the second is magnificent. It has an aroma of fruit and flowers and a pure, sweet taste that instantly explains why Jamaican Blue Mountain coffee is so highly prized. But the five remaining samples are all lackluster by comparison. They taste flat and boring. But all seven will end up in some blend of Jamaican Blue Mountain coffee.

Too bad you can't buy just the very best Blue Mountain coffee, we comment to a group of restaurant owners at a party in Kingston. An elegant woman quietly takes us aside and gives us the name and address of Alex Twyman. "He's a renegade," she says. "Go see him and have him make you a cup of coffee. He is the only grower in Jamaica who ages his coffee. He has the best coffee in Jamaica."

We are intrigued enough to make the tortuous trip back up the mountain to find Twyman. We arrive at sunset and knock on his door unannounced, since he doesn't have a phone. He and his wife Dorothy are sitting in their modest living room looking out over the red and silver clouds and the silhouetted mountain peaks. Directly below the living room window, the mountain takes a frighteningly steep drop. All along the mountainside, coffee trees reflect the dying sunlight.

London-born Twyman has lived in Jamaica for 35 years. He makes a living as a surveyor and is notorious for his independent thinking. "Would you like a cup of coffee?" he asks us. As he makes a pot, he begins to tell us the strange tale of international politics.

"The Japanese make all the money on Jamaican coffee," he says. They buy 90 percent of the entire crop at $7.50 a pound. The Jamaican Coffee Board pays the farmers about half that much. Then the Japanese roast the coffee in Tokyo and sell it for $60 a pound."

Twyman finds this arrangement crazy. "It's a form of Japanese colonialism," he thunders. "I'm required by law to sell to the coffee board at whatever price they choose to pay, regardless of the value of the product in the world market." He feels his plantation produces the very highest quality beans, and he wants to sell them under his own estate label instead of having them blended with lesser beans from other Blue Mountain areas.

The tiny room is beginning to fill with the rich, toasty aroma of fresh coffee. "Because of the microclimate up here, my beans take ten to eleven months to get from the blossom to the picking stage. The average is five months. I get a larger, harder bean because it takes so long to mature," he says.

In the early eighties, Twyman applied for a license to process and roast his own beans and sell them directly to buyers in Japan and the United States. The coffee board refused. That's when the stubborn Englishman started to age his coffee.

"I didn't set out to age my coffee; it was pure bloody-mindedness," he says. "I just told the Coffee Board to get stuffed." Twyman stopped selling his coffee beans to the coffee board in 1982. He puts the beans in storage in a warehouse in Kingston, hoping for the day when he could finally get a license to sell it direct. The intense smell of the coffee is starting to drive us crazy.

Twyman goes on to explain about aging. He had started to worry about the effects of storage on his coffee beans. So he did a little research. And he discovered that aged coffee was once a highly prized commodity. In both Venezuela and Sumatra, coffee beans aged for five years or more command a premium price. "We discovered that aging enhances the flavor of coffee. It mellows it," Twyman says.

Twyman's wife, Dorothy, comes to our rescue, gently reminding her husband that we are all waiting to taste some coffee. He hands us each a cup. Although we usually take cream and sugar, we drink this coffee black. The fragrance is fruity in the way that fine chocolate can smell fruity. Although the coffee is medium-roasted and brewed strong, the flavor is sweet and round and mellow all the way to the back of the throat. It is a spectacular cup of coffee.

"This is not your everyday cup of coffee," says Twyman, grinning. "This is the kind of coffee you serve after dinner with your best cognac."

And so the mystique of Jamaican Blue Mountain coffee lives on. Yes, coffee really can be that good. In fact, Twyman's coffee would be a bargain at thirty-five dollars a pound. And if Twyman ever gets his way, it may someday sell in your local coffee shop for even more than that.

But for now Alex Twyman is sitting on tens of thousands of pounds of the finest coffee beans in the world, probably the only aged Blue Mountain coffee in existence. And under Jamaican law he can't sell an ounce of it.

Dorothy returns with the pot. "Anybody for a refill?"

Ratbite Coffee

Keble Munn

Keble Munn, the former government minister who owns the Mavis Bank Coffee Factory, likes to tell the story of the most highly prized coffee of them all. "Ratbite coffee" is made from the beans bitten off the trees by rats. The rats go after the biggest, ripest, juiciest coffee berries, and then leave the beans behind. Farmers gather these up and process them separately to produce a very small amount of prime coffee for personal use.

Hardwar Gap

Clinging to a cliff, an elegant restaurant called the Gap offers one of the most hair-raising vistas in Jamaica. From the back deck you could practically parachute into downtown Kingston.

The Gap restaurant

The hills around the restaurant are part of the Hollywell Forest Park, an area with an annual rainfall of over one hundred inches. The jungle-like climate makes the park a favorite visiting place for naturalists, who come to appreciate the more than five hundred kinds of ferns, hanging plants, and orchids that grow here. The Gap is a favorite stopover after hikes through the mountain mist forest.

On this Sunday afternoon, Jay is playing guest chef for a special dinner put on by the restaurant's owner, his Aunt Gloria Palomino. A crowd of well-dressed food lovers have made the trek up the mountain in the rain to try Jay's cooking. Relegated to the role of assistant chef, I have spent my day chopping and peeling. Jay's pork loin with rosemary jerk rub and field green salad with crunchy noodles and nasturtiums are a big hit.

We picked the rosemary for the jerk rub in the nearby rain forest, and plucked the nasturtium blossoms from the Gap's garden. Although these are not traditional Jamaican recipes, they represent the wave of the future in Jamaican cooking. Visiting chefs from innovative Jamaican restaurants drop by during our dinner to talk with Jay about some of the new things they're doing with traditional Jamaican ingredients. Mei-Nan Lee-Sang, the chef from Temple Hall in Kingston, brings dessert, a wonderful tamarind soufflé which we enjoy with some of Twyman's aged Blue

Mountain coffee. After dessert, we say goodbye to our guests and retire to Aunt Gloria's to talk about food with a fascinating group of affluent Jamaicans.

"You've got to put all the good stuff no one knows about in your Jamaican cookbook," a jolly character named Dr. Barnaby tells us. "You've got to tell people about things like stinking toe!"

"Stinking toe?" we ask in amazement. Now everyone is talking at once, telling us about the weird Jamaican tree fruit known as stinking toe. Stinking toe looks like a large brown human toe, and its husk smells

An outdoor cooking range

as bad as its name suggests. Inside, a white powder that looks like confectioner's sugar is scraped from the fruit's chambers. It is eaten on the spot by children, and sometimes used to make a custard ice cream. That's right, stinking toe ice cream!

Now in full form, the crowd begins listing the unusual foods that Jamaican cookbooks always overlook. Byne pears and byne spears are cactus flower buds, which are often used like okra in pepperpot soup in the desert regions of St. Elizabeth, they point out. And who, they want to know, writes about asham, the cassava crumbs scraped from bammies that are made into a porridge? Tell people that cashew fruit and almond skins are turned into preserves after the nuts are removed, they demand. And that the seed of the guinep fruit can be roasted like a chestnut. "We used to eat green mangoes as a vegetable at my house," someone says. The list of unusual Jamaican delicacies goes on and on.

We are amazed by the seemingly endless variety of Jamaican cuisine. The abundance of little-known tropical fruits on this little island is awe-inspiring. We conclude the evening by promising to go hunting for some stinking toe and to include a recipe for stinking toe ice cream in our cookbook (see the recipe on page 206).

Faiths Pen

There's nothing charming about fast-food restaurants crowded together by a highway—until you see Faiths Pen. Here, along the side of the mountain road that crosses Jamaica from the city of Kingston to the beach resort of Ocho Rios, is the most engaging strip of highway fast food joints we've ever seen. Twenty-two stalls stand here side by side, and in each one someone is cooking up a unique version of Jamaican food to go.

We pull the car over and begin to wander up and down the row of stalls, buying a whole fried fish from one, a piece of jerk pork from another. We are trying to take in the whole experience in a few minutes. With the stall owners aggressively hawking their specialties and the trucks roaring by on the highway a few feet away, the effect is utter bedlam.

Each little eatery has a sign proudly display-ing its name. There's Sparrow's One Stop, Shortie's Place, Little John Cafe, Shut's Night and Day, and our favorite, Johnny Cool #1. We count five jerk shacks, three soup kitchens, and one organic juice and root tonic outlet. The other joints offer a hodgepodge of meals and snacks. Many of the proprietors stand in front of their shacks, grilling meat and fish on oil-drum barbecues. Jay and I each eat a pile of jerk, a lot of fish, and some arcane items like cow cod soup, which is made from a bull's testicles. It is actually quite tasty.

But as good as the food may be, Faiths Pen is in one way like any other fast-food operation—you're not encouraged to hang around. In fact, at Faiths Pen there aren't even any tables. So we load up the car and push on across the mountains.

Kingston

Our car swerves to avoid a crowd of pedestrians spilling from the side-walk. They carry groceries, children, and laundry as they swell the street crossing. At the stoplight, the car windows are crowded with hawkers trying to sell us cigarettes, newspapers, and chewing gum. Reggae music blares from car radios and boom boxes. The street signs are missing, car horns are blaring, and the traffic is intense. By the side of the road a man is sleeping in the dense foliage underneath a riotous stand of banana trees, while beside him a large crowd waits for a bus.

Kingston is a river of humanity that's overflowing its banks—seven hundred thousand people crowded together in a city that's too small to hold them all. And every day more people pour in from the country-side, looking for their fame and fortune. There's a crackling tension in the air that we haven't felt anywhere else in Jamaica. Like any big city, Kingston is as exciting as it is intimidating.

We start our mornings in Kingston at the Constant Spring Market, watching the produce vendors setting up their wares. The Scotch bonnet peppers, bananas, and pumpkins look familiar by now. We don't find any surprises in the market, and we begin to realize how much more produce costs here in the city.

After spending time in the nearby Blue Mountain coffee planta-tions, we're surprised to discover that, with all of Kingston's bustling commercialism, there aren't many places to get a cup of coffee. Even though it's one of the country's most famous exports it seems to play little part in the daily life of Jamaicans. Coffee may be hard to find, but we certainly don't have any trouble finding "patties."

A patty is a kind of meat pie that's usually filled with ground beef. Patties are everywhere in Kingston, and they are uniquely suited to the frenetic urban lifestyle. You don't need a table or a knife and fork to eat patties; they are the perfect meal for eating on the run. The name is said to come from the French word *pâté*, since patties usually have a finely ground beef filling. But beef is not the only thing you'll find stuffed into the patties in Kingston. A popular restaurant chain called Mother's features vegetable patties, and upscale restaurants make shrimp pat-ties. Jay has even experimented with wild boar patties. (See the patty recipes on pages 88-90).

The other food we see a lot of in Kingston is fish. Whole fried fish is sold by the side of the road all over town. We stop in for dinner at a restaurant called the Fish Place. The Fish Place consists of picnic tables under a roof; there aren't any walls. It's a fun and funky place to sample fried fish and the soup Jamaicans call fish tea.

Calling any kind of liquid "tea" is a custom left over from the days of British rule. Fish tea is a clear fish soup. Sometimes just the stock is drunk as a beverage, but most often it's consumed the way the Fish Place serves it—in a bowl with a lot of fish and vegetables. The fish is served bones and all, so it's a messy dish to eat. But with the profusion of fresh fish in Jamaica, you can usually count on a delicious meal when you order a bowl of this "tea" (see the recipe on page 98).

But Kingston has a lot more to offer food lovers than fish and patties. Within this sprawling urban scene are islands of calm refinement where Kingston's elite enjoy magnificent meals. The most impressive restaurant we visited was Temple Hall, where Jay's sister, Valery, hosted a get-together for Jay's birthday.

We toasted Jay with French champagne and ate a sumptuous meal, beneath an arbor of passion-fruit trees, on the patio of this elegant mansion. Smoked marlin (see the recipe on page 84) in puff pastry was one of the most interesting dishes we tried at Temple Hall.

Temple Hall's innovative chef, a beautiful young woman named Mei-Nan Lee-Sang, is known for such unusual dishes as jerked ackee pasta and a dessert called tamarind soufflé. The food at Temple Hall features elegant, fashionable dishes made with the finest Jamaican ingredients—a sort of haute Jamaican cuisine.

At the Devonshire restaurant in Kingston's famous Devon House, we had another sort of experience we won't forget—a Jamaican drinking experience. Under the trees on the patio we listened to a jazz band and ordered cocktails from the huge list of Jamaican rum drinks. We toasted with Devon Duppies, Pawpaws, and a drink named after a female pirate, Ann Bonnie. We sampled more kinds of rum than any of us remember. Once again, Valery served as designated driver, escorting her stumbling charges safely home.

Old Harbour

The Victorian iron clock in the middle of the road is the landmark that announces you've arrived in downtown Old Harbour. It's a quaint old town, but we're not here to sightsee. We're here for the two things Old Harbour is most famous for—fish and the strange cassava pancakes called bammies.

As we pull over in front of the stands where the "fish ladies" peddle their fried parrot fish and snapper, the commotion begins. Women are handing us fried fish through the car windows before we can even get out the doors.

We smile politely and start asking questions. A heavyset black woman with a kerchief on her head looks just like the Aunt Jemima on the syrup bottles. Her name is Sonja Mendez, "Tete" to her friends—and we are definitely her friends. As we stand admiring her wares, Tete announces that she is my girlfriend. Her romantic interest in me is strictly mercenary. She is trying to outmaneuver the other fish ladies and make a big sale. She figures I look like a big eater.

But Tete loses all interest in me as soon as she lays eyes on Jay. It's not Jay's youthful stature or curly hair that Tete is impressed by, though; it's his chef's whites. Jay appeared on a TV talk show that morning to discuss Jamaican cooking, and he hasn't had time to change. Tete runs her fingers over the colorfully embroidered name above Jay's breast pocket. All of a sudden, the competition over which fish we are going to buy is completely forgotten.

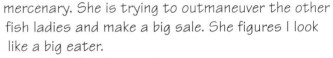

Tete is of the strong opinion that she should have a job working as a cook in Jay's restaurant back in Texas. She grabs Jay's sleeve and immediately begins to make the most forceful job application I have ever witnessed. She is the best cook we will ever meet, she assures us. As her resume she offers her exclusive recipes for oxtail soup, peas and rice, and curry goat. But her most stunning performance is her recitation of the recipe for mannish water.

Tete Mendez tells Jay about mannish water

Mannish water is part soup, part legendary elixir. It's made from the head of a goat, and it's served to Jamaican grooms on their wedding nights to boost their virility. When a guy orders mannish water in a restaurant, the waitress gets a gleam in her eye and asks him if he has a big date.

When it's well made, mannish water is a very tasty soup. But Tete's recipe seems to focus more on the magic than the flavor. Her voice goes into a lower register as she summons up her spell: "Boil de goat head and chop de green bananas," she says, acting out the chopping.

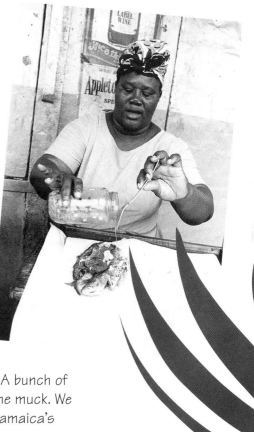

"You peel the bananas first, right?" asks Jay.

"No! You cut the peel up small and you put that in, too!" bellows Tete. "Make it strong!" She flexes her massive arm in front of her. We try to copy down Tete's mannish water recipe, but we are so mesmerized by her performance that we can barely take our eyes off of her. This isn't a recipe, it's a magic incantation.

Finally, there is only one way to escape the Old Harbour fish ladies. We buy up all the fried fish in sight, drench the whole mess in hot sauce, and sit down on the curb to have a feast.

The fish ladies gave us directions. But the mud-filled front yard and the humble house don't look right. Could this really be the place where the best bammies in Jamaica are made? It's an unpainted house just a few blocks from the fish ladies' stand in the town of Old Harbour. A bunch of kids come out to stare at us as we fumble our way through the muck. We knock on the door and get a strange look from Joy Manson, Jamaica's reigning bammie queen.

Yes, she's the one who makes the bammies, she tells us. Joy is the stepmother of one of Jamaica's most famous DJ's, a reggae-rocker who goes by the name of the Bammie Man. The Bammie Man once made bammies here with his stepmom, and he still sells them. But nowadays Joy does all the cooking.

We are more than a little embarrassed to be standing here at Joy's front door bothering her, and we don't know what to do about our muddy shoes.

"Well, can we watch you make some bammies?" Jay bravely suggests. "Come around the back and I'll show you," Joy offers. We are relieved that we don't have to enter her house with muddy shoes. Jay and I walk around to Joy's backyard, where she has her bammie griddle set up under a lean-to roof.

"Bammie Queen" Joy Manson demonstrates a bammie mold

Bammies are a strange food indeed. They are thick pancakes made of pressed cassava. The grated cassava has the consistency of grated potatoes, but it tastes sweeter. The cassava pancakes are compressed in a mold, so that they are thick and dense. Hot off the griddle, they are delicious. The outside is toasty crisp, and the dense cassava is steaming and moist.

But more often than not a bammy is served cold. And when it gets stale, a bammy can have all the culinary charm of a hockey puck. And the process of making bammies is downright frightening. The grated cassava must be pressed hard to remove as much liquid as possible. Why? Bcause the juice that is pressed out of the raw cassava is a deadly poison!

Joy Manson has learned the hard way to keep the goats that wander her backyard a safe distance away while she pours out the juice she has squeezed from her cassava gratings. "Sometime a goat get loose and drink some o' dat water and den he go two, three steps and fall over," Joy laughs.

Joy places the iron rings onto the hot griddle and presses the cassava gratings in hard to mold the pancakes. After turning the bammies, she pops them out of the mold and scrapes off the coarse crumbs to leave a smooth surface. The crumbs, called asham, are made into a porridge for the children's breakfast.

We buy a few of Joy's hot bammies and thank her for her time, but before we leave we ask her about the rhythmic beating, like a hammer on wood, coming from the shed in her backyard. She takes us over and introduces us to her father-in-law, the original Bammie Man, the man who taught Joy how to make bammies.

An elderly black man, he is sitting on the floor in the darkened shed, splitting tiny scraps of wood with an ax. "What's this for?" asks Jay, picking up a chunk of wood and sniffing it. "That's strong back, for my tonic," the man replies. Suddenly we realize that all these little scraps are carefully collected roots, barks and woods that will be brewed into "tonics," Jamaica's folk medicines.

Jay squats down and sorts through the debris, holding up each scrap and asking its name. The old man barely looks up as he replies. "Peanut root, chaney root, strong back, blood wiss, nerve wiss, popgun root, chewstick, bissy root, khus khus root, ramgoat dash-along…" He has a story about each root and its powers. People come from miles around to get his tonics, we are told. We are looking at Old Harbour's leading pharmacist.

Greyground, Manchester

Under the eaves of the building, out of the driving rain, a dozen black women sit and giggle while we snap their pictures. "Hey, take my picture!" one insists, and soon we are swamped with portrait orders.

The women are happy to be distracted from the tedious job of cleaning ackee—mountains of it. We are visiting a business known locally as "the ackee factory." Mr. Ashman is the owner of the Caribbean Exotic Food Company, as it is more formally titled, and he is taking us on a tour.

Cleaning ackee

The canning line looks like any other small canning operation, it's what's in the cans that's strange. The yellow ackee fruits with their lobes and fissures look like tiny brains. Ashman is lecturing us about how unfair it is that he can't export his canned ackee to the United States. There is a huge market for the product in the West Indian grocery stores of Miami, Houston, and Atlanta. But the U.S. government bars the product from being imported.

The reason for this ban is that the aril of the ackee is poisonous in the wrong stage of bloom. If the fruits are picked before the pods are fully opened or after they have gotten too ripe, ackee can be lethal. Every year a few cases of "Jamaica poisoning" are reported on the island.

Nevertheless, ackee and saltfish, a mixture of ackee and reconstituted salt cod, is one of the island's most popular dishes. The dish looks and tastes a little like scrambled eggs with fish in it.

Ashman has his own theory about why the U.S. government bars the import of his canned ackee. "It's the American egg producers that are behind this," he tells us. Ashman insists that the delicious and fat-free ackee is a healthier alternative to scrambled eggs, and that Americans would abandon their egg habit if only they could get his ackee. Who knows, maybe Ashman is right.

Ackee

Pickapeppa

In 1921, a sixteen-year old boy named Norman Nash began monopolizing his mother's kitchen. "I had to wait until he went to school to get into the kitchen," Mrs. Nash reportedly complained.

But Mrs. Nash's patience was eventually very richly rewarded. Young Norman Nash's experiments yielded one of the most famous bottled sauces in the world—the sweet pepper sauce known as Pickapeppa.

In the early part of the century, every household in the farming region outside Mandeville made its own homemade tomato sauce from the small local tomatoes grown there. Norman Nash's now-legendary version contains tomatoes, onions, cane vinegar, mangoes, raisins, tamarinds, peppers, and spices.

"It was just something I always wanted to do," the soft-spoken Nash told reporters years later. Rhonda Jackson, a relative of Nash, designed the famous green, gold, and red label with a picture of a parrot on a pepper branch. Norman hired friends and neighbors to grow the produce for him. By 1922, the operation had become so large that it was moved to its present home in Shooter's Hill.

Today Pickapeppa Sauce is sold in 41 countries around the world. At the Pickapeppa factory, thousands of wooden casks hold the treasured sauce, which ages one year in oak before it is released.

Pickapeppa sauce is so popular in Jamaica that when a longshoreman's strike halted production, people began hoarding the sauce, causing a worldwide shortage that lasted for two years.

Mandeville

After spending the night with Jay's aunt and uncle, Ralph and Hilda James, we sit down to a huge Mandeville breakfast. The table is spread with johnny cakes, boiled green bananas, sweet corn porridge, ackee and saltfish, roasted breadfruit, coffee, and orange juice. Just the sustenance we need to carry us through a long day of—well, eating.

Jay and Valerie's aunt and uncle James are prosperous business owners in Mandeville. I am somewhat puzzled because, whereas Jay and Valery look white, their aunt and uncle are dark-skinned. Jay laughs, explaining that within his extended Jamaican family are Welsh, Africans, Indians, Chinese, and a few nationalities they haven't figured out yet. This blend of backgrounds within a single family is typical of modern Jamaica. This island is one place where people of different races have answered positively Rodney King's question, "Can't we all just get along?"

"Out of many, one people" is the Jamaican national motto, and this blending of cultures explains a lot about Jamaican food. At this breakfast table alone we see bananas and citrus, fruits introduced by the Spanish; breadfruit, which was brought here by the British from the South Pacific; salt fish and ackee, a dish invented by Jamaica's black slaves; and corn porridge, an indigenous food of the New World. "Out of many, one cuisine" might be the country's culinary motto.

Spur Tree Hill

The gamey aroma of goat meat punches you in the nose all along the twisting road down the mountainside. Spur Tree Hill Road, just outside Mandeville, is Jamaica's most famous stretch of road for curry goat lovers.

We pull over at Alex's Curry Goat Spot, a tiny restaurant with a big reputation. There are four tables in the place and three chairs at the counter. The chipped tile floor is lit by a bare bulb hanging from a wire.

This little restaurant, which Arthur Alexander opened 24 years ago, is probably the most popular place to eat curry goat on the island. The secret of Arthur's success, and the secret of all great curry goat, is simple—freshly-killed goat meat. Every morning at 6 a.m., for as long as he can remember, Arthur has killed a goat.

When he's done with his butchering, the goat's head and feet and the tripe go into the pressure cooker to make mannish water. The rest of the meat becomes curry goat. A plate of curry goat with rice and boiled banana goes for 53 Jamaican dollars, about two bucks U.S.

First we take a tour of the facility—a tiny home kitchen with huge pots of mannish water and curry goat cooking on the little stove. The cook, Cherry Baker, dictates the recipe for curry goat while Jay scribbles it down (see the recipe on page 127). Cherry uses the pressure cooker to cook the goat meat until it is tender, and adds the other ingredients later.

Finally, Jay and I sit down at the counter and order some curry goat. We dig into our big plates of food, carefully fishing out the splintered bones that are always present in the authentic version of the dish. The curry goat is excellent. Although the smell of the meat is strong, it is surprisingly mild-tasting. The curry sauce, however, is not; it has a spicy, lingering afterburn. I order my first Jamaican ginger beer to wash down the spicy curry. One large swallow later, I'm in shock. The ginger beer is hotter than the curry.

Goshen

Compared to the barren scenery of Mandeville's bauxite mining district, the drive down Spur Tree Hill is spectacular. The flat, fertile valley of St. Elizabeth Parish spreads out for miles. When we reach the bottom of the hill, we drive through vast cattle ranches and farms. The landscape reminds Jay and me of the wide-open spaces back home in Texas.

Near Goshen we pull over at an open-air restaurant called Kitchen Garden, and sit under a thatched roof shelter built around an ackee tree. The restaurant is aptly named: Coconut, mango, papaya, avocado, banana, and breadfruit trees are growing all around us. Out back we visit the garden, where the restaurant owners cultivate pumpkins, sweet potatoes, onions, squash, and herbs. The driveway is lined with flowering cactus, birds of paradise, and purple, yellow, and white hibiscus. Even the tables have little potted flowers on them.

In the beautiful sunny weather, this is an idyllic stopover, even if the mannish water we order is a little disappointing. It has been reheated, and the broth is thin and watery. The beer is cold, though, and the scenery makes up for a lot.

Middle Quarters

Bamboo Avenue is a three-mile stretch of road shaded by the largest grove of bamboo we've ever seen. Planted along both sides of the road, the enormous bamboo trees converge overhead to form a cathedral ceiling.

At the other end of Bamboo Avenue is the little village of Middle Quarters, famous for its "pepper-shrimp ladies." The ladies sit along the roadside holding up their bags of shrimp. If you stop the car, they converge on you, "higgling" for your business.

Pepper shrimp are actually made with a kind of crawfish or freshwater shrimp. They are boiled in a brine spiked with Scotch bonnet peppers. We buy a large bag of pepper shrimp and carry it into the nearest bar, where we eat the whole mess with a couple of cold Red Stripes. The bartender has her own theories on where and when the best pepper shrimp can be found, and we take her advice on which lady to get some more from. Jay and I flip a coin to see who will go back out to the road to buy it.

Black River

The elegant Georgian-style houses that line the main street of the sleepy little town of Black River remind you that this was once a bustling port and commercial center. Fustic and logwood, two trees once used to produce commercial dyes, were the mainstays of Black River's economy. Today these natural dyes have been replaced by synthetic products, and the once-thriving port of Black River has grown quiet.

In the early afternoon, we arrive at the home of Jay's cousins, Sheila and Michael James, who live not far from the town's center. After greeting us with a cup of tea, Sheila and Michael head back to work.

With an afternoon to kill, Jay and I hop back into the car to explore the neighborhood. Driving along the beach to Parrotee Point, we pass a tiny "store," where a couple of men are sitting out front playing dominoes. Jay looks back, and suddenly demands that we stop the car. In the backyard of this store, Jay has spotted a five-gallon coconut oil tin propped on three rocks over an open fire. "That's what we're looking for!" he hollers.

Behind the counter we find a lovely young woman named Myrna Bryan. "Is that mannish water you're cooking out back?" Jay asks her. She shyly admits that it is, and we all go out back to take a look.

The best mannish water is always found cooking in a five gallon coconut oil tin over an open fire.

"The best mannish water is always cooking in a five-gallon tin in somebody's backyard," Jay whispers to me. I'm skeptical. But the soup is thick and full of "spinners," Jay's favorite kind of dumplings, and I have to admit it looks pretty good.

We ask Myrna to sell us a couple of cups of soup, and we sit down inside to eat it. It is the best mannish water either of us has ever tasted. It is thickened with dasheen and cho-cho squash, which have been boiled until they've fallen apart. The goat meat is cleaned of all bone and gristle and is perfectly tender, and the dumplings are delicious, too.

So this is what mannish water is about. (See the recipe on page 109.)

Black River Market

People are sleeping in the vegetables, sprawled out on top of bales of callaloo and bunches of bananas. Meanwhile, others unload trucks of produce in the eerie light of bare electric bulbs. It's Friday night in the Black River market. Saturday morning is the region's market day.

Vendors truck their goods in from all over the island on Friday night. Then they neatly stack their produce, cover it with canvas tarps and try to get some sleep. The contrast between the sleeping figures and the vendors who are still frantically unloading makes a strange scene.

Berty Jones pours us some of his peanut root tonic

After we've looked around at the fruits and vegetables, we duck into a little beer stand owned by a man named Berty Jones. We order a couple of Red Stripes, but Berty has other ideas. Berty is known around the market as "the white beard man," and, unbeknownst to us, he makes a locally famous tonic called peanut wine.

Instead of the beers we've ordered, Berty sets up two glasses and gets down a bottle of his strange-looking potion. He pours us each a glass of peanut wine, saying, "Now this what you really need." Jay and I regard the tonic suspiciously. It was poured out of an old rum bottle and it has a lot of little chunks floating in it.

"What's this?" we ask.

"It's my peanut-root tonic," Berty says.

A couple of banana vendors, drinking Dragon Stout at the other end of the bar, are laughing now as we stare at the glasses and wonder what to do. "But what are these things floating in it?" we ask.

"It's peanuts!" Berty says impatiently.

By now it's obvious that we aren't going to go anywhere until we drink this stuff. So we both pick up our glasses and take a swallow. But you can't just swallow this tonic, you have to chew it first. The little chunks of peanuts would choke you otherwise. We expected the worst, but the tonic doesn't taste half bad. It's sweet and slightly alcoholic—

besides being chewy.

Now the guys down at the end of the bar are giving us the high sign and laughing hysterically. "You're going to make your girlfriend happy tonight," somebody says. Peanut root is evidently another of Jamaica's aids to virility. Jay and I joke that after the mannish water this afternoon and peanut wine tonight, the women of Jamaica may not be safe.

Berty allows that if we still want a beer we can have one. The peanut wine is on the house. But we should drink Dragon Stout instead of Red Stripe, he says, because it goes better with the peanut wine. After a couple of beers, I think that Jay's mind has definitely been affected by the tonic. He is dickering with Berty over the price of a bottle. Sure enough, we leave the market with our very own bottle of Berty's peanut wine. It will provide Valery with something to tease us about for the rest of the trip.

Miss
Lovena Braham
sells us a fish

The following morning we return to find the Black River Market in full swing. First we hit the fish department, where one of the most persuasive saleswomen we've ever met sells us a fish we don't need. Lovena Braham is an extraordinary fishmonger. Once we take her picture swinging her biggest fish by the tail, she becomes convinced that this giant pompano is destined for our dinner table. And Lovena is not a woman to be denied.

Carrying our fish, we stop at a fruit stall for a couple of gros michels to eat for breakfast. A gros michel is a kind of oversized banana that was once the most popular variety of banana in Jamaica, but nowadays it is getting rare. The gros michel was not as disease-resistant as other strains, and it was almost completely wiped out by "yellow leaf" disease. It is sweet and custardy, one of the tastiest bananas we've ever had.

39

With our pet pompano, we climb into the car and leave Black River on our last day together. We've decided to have a little fun swimming and exploring YS Falls. It takes more than an hour to negotiate the washed-out dirt roads through the papaya orchards that lead to the entrance of this spectacular series of waterfalls. But the drive is worth it. The falls are on the YS River. The odd name is probably a corruption of the Welsh word *wyess*, which means "winding."

First, we make a deal with the bartender. We give him our pompano and convince him to fire up the grill out back while we go swimming. Then we climb aboard the little tractor-pulled jitney that takes visitors up through the jungle to the waterfalls.

Some people just come to look at the huge surge of green water thundering down the mountain, but the more adventurous brave the currents for a swing on the rope swing or a view of the caves behind the highest falls. The three of us, apparently in the latter category, are soon being led by a swimming guide back behind a curtain of water and up into the rocks behind the waterfall. The air is so misty, it's hard to breathe.

The pompano, marinated in lime juice and papaya puree during our swim, tastes great hot off the grill with a couple of Red Stripes. (See the recipe on page 137.)

From here, Jay and Valery head back to Kingston and I go on to Negril for an eating tour of the posh hotels and luxury resorts that have made Jamaica famous as a tourist destination.

It's sad to say good-bye, but we're pretty exhausted, and I'm looking forward to visiting a beach or two. But then I realize I'm not just saying good-bye to Jay and Valery. I'm also saying good-bye to the real Jamaica.

While I'm looking forward to the soft life at the resorts, I know I won't be getting any more opportunities to talk to characters like Berty the peanut-wine maker or Lovena the pompano pusher. I'll miss them.

Half Moon Bay Resort

Grand Lido, Negril

As I arrive at the Grand Lido, I am greeted with a glass of French champagne. The huge domed ceiling of the foyer is topped with a skylight that fills the room with sensuous tropical light. On a round table in the middle of the room, an arrangement of exquisite flowers radiates color.

Jay and Valery have dropped me off here in Negril, where my mission is to visit a few of Jamaica's premiere luxury resorts and collect recipes. It's a tough assignment, but somebody's got to do it.

I have barely been at the Grand Lido for an hour before I am summoned to join a cocktail cruise. A small motor launch picks us up at the dock and zooms us over to the Grand Lido's magnificent yacht, the Zein.

The Zein is a 145-foot restored antique motor yacht. Everywhere you look, rich-grained woods and shiny brass ooze old-fashioned elegance. Aristotle Onassis gave the ship as a wedding present to Prince Rainier and Princess Grace who spent their honeymoon on board. The ship has an enormous master bedroom, a state room with a dining table for twelve, and a full living room with a wet bar.

We spend two hours cruising around the harbor drinking French champagne and eating canapés. If Jay and Valery could see me now!

We eat crab in puff pastry, snails in puff pastry, and a delicious tamarind shrimp.

The next day I visit the Grand Lido's main dining room. The buffet lunch features ackee and saltfish, grilled red snapper, callaloo, and a lot of other Jamaican specialties along with smoked salmon and bagels and the expected tourist offerings.

I spend the rest of the day enjoying the Grand Lido's beach and visiting the bartenders. The only hazard in hanging around the beachside bars at the Grand Lido (besides getting tipsy) is the yellow jackets. The bartenders use so many different varieties of sweet tropical fruits that they can't keep the wasps away.

But hanging around to watch the bartenders make drinks is worth the risk. The Grand Lido's bartenders have invented more unique cocktails than I've ever seen in one place before. They serve cocktails made with breadfruit, cocktails made with pumpkin and cocktails made with almond fruit (see the recipes on pages 52-72).

These bartenders are just as inventive with their nonalcoholic beverages as they are with rum drinks. The Sour Mup Mup, for instance, is a nonalcoholic cocktail made with sweetsop and soursop. These two Jamaican fruits have a custardy pulp that makes a rich, creamy fruit drink (see the recipe on page 72).

After a day at the beach, I visit the Grand Lido's French restaurant, Placere, for dinner. My first shock is the discovery that a jacket is required in the restaurant. I didn't bring a dinner jacket, so I am kindly lent one. The next surprise is the menu. Along with Chausson of Duck Confit, Dialogue of Nigiri and Maki Sushi, and Cake of Standing Jumbo Prawn, the appetizer section includes Seafood Symphony Panache of Marinated Kiwi Clams, Native Smoked Marlin and Savory Cheesecake with Buttons of Citrus Dip, and Trio of Caviars presented in Abstract Fashion.

Most of the entrées are a little more familiar: New York steaks, swordfish, lamb roast, and veal chops. But I choose "Supreme of Wild Pintelle [a Jamaican game bird] Filled with Saffron Langouste Mousseline in Wine Leaves, Poached Gently in a Spicy Chardonnay Nectar, Garnished with Skin Crackles and Multi Herbed Yogurt Cream." The dish is pleasantly rich and very delicate. The restaurant is a treat, but it's definitely more French than Jamaican.

It's tough to leave the modern luxury and impeccable taste of the Grand Lido, but, as Jimmy Cliff would say, "I have many rivers to cross."

Half Moon Golf, Tennis, and Beach Club, Half Moon Bay

The white columns and Georgian architecture tell you as you walk in the front door that the Half Moon is a resort from a more romantic era. Inside the front hall, the dark wood paneling, old-fashioned tile floors, and antique furniture confirm the first impression. With a lot of leather club chairs, slowly revolving ceiling fans, and waiters in immaculate white uniforms who are dying to get you a rum and tonic, the club looks like a leftover from the heyday of the British Empire.

The Seagrape Terrace is the center of attention. It's a huge patio, complete with gazebo band shell and shaded by seagrape and palm trees. It's also the main dining room and dance floor. A more formal restaurant known as the Sugarmill is a short distance away.

Half Moon is named for the perfect crescent beach around which the resort is built. If you're lucky, you get a room in one of the little white plantation-style houses down the long sidewalk that runs along the beach. There you get your own little patio with a picnic table and your own private stretch of sand complete with chaise lounges. I get lucky.

Half Moon has a Robert Trent Jones golf course, tennis courts, and 17 swimming pools. But I hardly ever leave the terrace—it is a great place for people watching. In the evening, the throb of the dance music makes it hard to go anywhere else.

At dinnertime, I sit at a table with a view of the beach and sample Half Moon's hot and hearty pepperpot soup. It's meaty and thick with a lot of fresh callaloo, like a spinach soup with meat and peppers. (Various pepperpot recipes can be found on pages 105-107.)

Room Service at
Half Moon Bay

Montego Bay

Young thyme salesmen and pineapple vendors keep me company in Montego Bay's market. The town is a great place to go shopping for reggae tapes and other souvenirs, but the vegetable market is quite small. One the way back, I stop at the Native Restaurant and meet the owner, Boris Reid.

Boris encourages me to try his favorite cocktail, a spicy shot of pimento dram over ice. If you like the taste of allspice, this is quite a drink. It's hot and spicy and sweet, all at the same time. Then Boris and I get talking about how different the food is from region to region in Jamaica. He points to the case of dokono.

Dokono is a package of sweetened starch wrapped in a banana leaf, much like a Mexican tamale. The excellent dokono I am eating was made with cornmeal, Boris says (see the recipe on page 91). In the northeast, near Port Antonio, dokono is made with mashed green bananas, he tells me, and in the South near Mandeville, it's filled with a cassava mixture.

Boris goes on to describe how the climate of each part of Jamaica has produced a different kind of agriculture and therefore a different approach to the same cuisine. We talk about my favorite subject, hot peppers, as we admire the restaurant's incredible view of the sea.

After our talk, I am honored when Boris has his chef prepare me a special bowl of Scotch bonnet pepper sauce to go with my fried fish. "I don't usually put this out on the table because people can hurt themselves with it, but I think you'll like it," he says with a wink. It is a cane vinegar-based sauce with peppers, onions, and ginger—very tasty and very hot (see the recipe on page 145).

Round Hill

The walls of the bar are covered with old black and white photos of presidents, movie stars and royalty: Katherine Hepburn, Cole Porter, Grace Kelly. Over there is the piano Noel Coward used to play when he stayed here. That was Jack Kennedy's favorite villa. Round Hill was their hangout in Jamaica, and is still one of the most exclusive and stylish hideaways in the world. The grilled marlin isn't bad, either.

I have stopped by for dinner at just the right time. Someone has caught a marlin, and the cooks are tossing inch-thick steaks onto a hot grill and drizzling them with a little citrus-pepper sauce. I enjoy the juiciest fish steak I've ever eaten (see the recipe on page 139).

Montego Bay musicians

If I felt strange without a dinner jacket at Grand Lido, I feel even stranger here at Round Hill. Men in black ties and women in haute-couture evening dresses are gathering for cocktails inside. But it is still early, and my Hawaiian shirt is fine for dinner on the terrace. I finish dinner with a cup of Blue Mountain coffee and tell my dinner companions about a guy I met in the Blue Mountains who makes the best cup of coffee in the world.

Sandals' Royal Caribbean

I feel like a third wheel at the couples-only resort, Sandals. Everybody I see, lounging around the hot tub or sitting at the bar, looks so lovey-dovey. "I'm only here for dinner," I want to reassure all the happy pairs. Chef Louis Bailey has invited me to sit in on a special dinner featuring native Jamaican dishes. I feel like I'm horning in on somebody's honeymoon.

We take a boat ride out to an island restaurant—Kokomo Island, it's called. The restaurant building looks like an Oriental palace. There are Jamaican dancers doing folk dances, costumed men beating Arawak drums, and a band playing calypso songs. It's quite a spectacle.

Our first course is a bammy filled with ackee au gratin; then comes a chicken consommé with fever grass (lemon grass). A salad of lettuce and a berry called a susumber follows. Like so many things I've eaten and drunk on this trip, the susumber is supposed to be an aphrodisiac. It looks like a big caper and tastes oddly sour.

Dip and Fall Back is the name of our excellent red snapper dish, a baked fish in a coconut sauce. Then there's an ortanique sherbet (an ortanique is an orange-tangerine hybrid) to clear our palate before the main course: a spicy jerk lobster (see the recipe on page 123). Dessert is a jelly coconut in a molded chocolate shell. The wonderful, pudding-like flesh of the baby coconut is a unique Jamaican treat.

Tryall Golf, Tennis and Beach Club

Tryall Great House, a plantation house built in 1834, sits on top of a hill and has a commanding view—of an incredible golf course. I should be paying more attention to the historic house and the Georgian antiques that furnish every room, but I am mesmerized by the golf course. It is one of the most impeccably groomed and imaginative layouts I've ever seen.

Others might not care that this course plays host to major international tournaments, or appreciate the seaside holes with waves breaking beside the greens, but I'm a golf junkie. In fact, if you didn't love golf, or love somebody who loves golf, you probably wouldn't decide to stay here. Yes, Tryall has a great beach, a lot of tennis courts, and villas with antique furniture, like many other resorts. But, my lord, what a golf course.

From a table beside the bar, I can open the window and watch a foursome approach the green far below. Finally, something else catches my attention. I think I smell food. Gerard Resnick, the executive chef, has put out a spread of appetizers.

I sample my way around the buffet, returning again and again to something Resnick calls Escoveitch Yellow Fin Tuna. These spicy yellow fin tuna tidbits on skewers are addictive. They go well with another innovative appetizer, one he calls Callaloo Rundown on Fried Plantains. A thick spicy purée of the Jamaican greens called callaloo is spooned neatly in the center of fried plantain slices (see the recipe on page 92).

I carry a large plate of tuna skewers and plantain canapés back to the bar window to watch the boys putt out. I wish I could hang around and play a few rounds of golf, but this is my "last resort."

In the week I've spent seeing how the better half lives, I've seen another side of Jamaican cooking. While Jamaican resort food lacks the fun and funky authenticity of a roadside goat curry stand or a jerk shack, it has its own charm. It's interesting to see how a French chef deals with Jamaican ingredients as they do at Grand Lido, and how down-home foods like ackee, plantain, and callaloo can be dressed up in exciting presentations like Sandals' ackee au gratin and Tryall's callaloo rundown on fried plantains.

In fact, along with such great restaurants as Kingston's Temple Hall, Jamaican resorts have pioneered the development of an upscale Jamaican cuisine. This new style of Jamaican cooking is an exciting part of the larger Caribbean cuisine movement that has been made popular in Miami by chefs like Allen Susser and Mark Militello.

A style which combines Caribbean ingredients with classical European cooking techniques seems natural in Jamaica. That kind of cultural fusion has been going on here for a long time. As the popularity of Caribbean cooking grows all over the world, the cross-pollination of Jamaican ingredients with new culinary techniques promises to produce some exciting new hybrids. Don't be surprised to see upscale Jamaican restaurants popping up all over.

But Jamaican resorts aren't just cooking upscale dishes. They do a pretty good job with classic Jamaican dishes like pepperpot and saltfish and ackee, too, so it is possible for tourists to get a good sampling of Jamaican cuisine without ever leaving their resorts.

Of course, food lovers who stay at Jamaican resorts will also want to take an expedition or two out to a restaurant or a jerk shack to meet the colorful characters and sample the native cooking that have made Jamaica famous. And I have no doubt their efforts will be richly rewarded.

On a plane above Jamaica

Looking out the window at the blue mountain peaks towering over the jungle-covered landscape, at the turquoise water, and at the endless beaches, I feel the sharp pang of parting. I feel as if I could have kept exploring Jamaica for the rest of my life.

But now I open a road map and start to remember all the places I've just been. And I realize how much ground we covered and how many things we ate in just two weeks. As I mark the map with a little dot at each of our stops, I have to admit that we really did a pretty good job of eating our way across Jamaica.

Of course, without Jay McCarthy's knowledge of the island and his memories of all the great things he grew up eating here, our odyssey wouldn't have been possible. And without Valery's fluent patois, we wouldn't have understood half of what people were trying to tell us. For me, the trip was the ultimate guided tour of a culture that would have otherwise remained a mystery.

But most of all, the trip gave us a righteous taste of Jamaican cooking. Our compliments to the chefs. And our thanks to all the kind people who took us into their kitchens and shared their recipes and their stories. Respect.

—Robb Walsh

Coffee man, at Mavis Bank

Chapter 2

Policemen, Shandies, and Drams

Jamaican Thirst-Quenchers

W hen you're stretched out in the sun on a palm-lined beach or beside the pool at one of Jamaica's plush resorts, admiring the well-tanned bodies, and listening to a reggae tune, one of the hardest questions you face is "What do you want to drink?"

First of all, of course, you have to try the most famous Jamaican drink of them all—a Red Stripe beer, also known as a "policeman" because the red stripe on the label looks like a Jamaican policeman's red sash. But after you've gotten that important experience out of the way, you'll be free to explore the rest of Jamaica's liquid bounty.

Jamaica's rums are among the finest in the world. Dark rums like Myer's are ideal for punch drinks. Golden rums like Appleton Estate, Sangster's Aged Rum, and Gold Label are best with lighter mixes. Gold Label, in particular, is a good sipping rum. To get the full effect of golden rum, try a shot on the rocks. Then start experimenting with the luscious rum and fruit-juice combinations.

The secret of Jamaican rum-and-juice drinks is not the quality of the rum alone. It's also the Jamaican fruits—guava, passion fruit, mango, and papaya—hanging from the trees waiting to be squeezed. These fresh fruits taste great with or without the rum. In fact, Jamaicans love to mix up blends of fresh fruit juices with tasty additives like mint or ginger. These are incredibly refreshing in the heat of the day.

Then there's Jamaican ginger beer. What a surprise this is! If you think you're about to take a swallow of something resembling American ginger ale, guess again. Jamaican ginger beer is spicy stuff indeed. And while you're drinking out of a bottle, don't miss Ting, the Jamaican grapefruit soda.

So what are you waiting for? Go find the bartender and tell him to fire up the blender.

Sugar Syrup (Simple Syrup)

Keep this handy for your tropical drinks.

1/2 cup sugar
1/2 cup water

Mix the sugar and water in a saucepan. Bring the mixture to a rapid boil. Simmer it for a minute or two, and let it cool.

Yields: 3/4 cup

Jamaican Rum Punch

This drink is a favorite at most of the resort hotels on the island. The recipe is easy to remember, because it rhymes: 1 of sour, 2 of sweet, 3 of strong, 4 of weak. If you can't remember the rhyme, don't make another batch yet!

1 of sour (fresh lime juice)
2 of sweet (Kelly strawberry syrup, or
    Simple Syrup with a little grenadine)
3 of strong (rums: Appleton, Sangster's,
    or Overproof rum, or the rum of your
    preference]
4 of weak (water and crushed ice)

The rhyme refers to "parts" of the ingredients. You can use empty rum bottles for measuring your "parts," as Jay's mom always does. Combine all the liquid ingredients in a punch bowl, add the ice, and stir well. Serve over chipped ice in 8-ounce glasses.

You can pour the leftover punch into the empty bottles, and store it in the refrigerator.

Yields: whatever amount you desire

Rum Runner

This one packs a punch. But what do you expect from a drink with three rums and two liqueurs?

1 ounce light rum
1 ounce Myer's dark rum
1/2 ounce Overproof white rum
1 1/2 ounces banana liqueur
1 ounce blackberry brandy
1/2 ounce grenadine
1 1/2 ounces lime juice
1 1/2 cups crushed ice

Combine all of the ingredients in a blender, and purée until the mixture is smooth. Pour it into tall rocks glasses, and garnish with lime wedges.

Serves 2

Jay's Awesome Pineapple Partyladas

Jay developed this recipe while trying to come up with a better margarita. But the flavor of pineapple blends far better with rum than it does with tequila, so Jay turned this into a piña colada recipe.

The drink is best if you start preparing it a week in advance, so the pineapples get permeated with the rum. The flavor is well worth the wait.

2 large, very ripe pineapples
2 ounces ginger root, coarsely chopped (skin included)
1/2 cup brown sugar
1 vanilla bean, split (or 1 teaspoon vanilla extract)
2 cups Myer's dark rum
1 cup Overproof white rum
2 cups Gold Label light rum
4 cups coconut milk (Coco Lopez or canned coconut milk can be substituted)

To soak the pineapple: Cut the top and bottom off the pineapple. With the skin on, cut lengthwise into a dozen slices. Place the slices in a glass pitcher or large glass jar. Add the ginger, the brown sugar, and vanilla bean. Add the rums. Cover the container tightly. Let the concoction stand at room temperature for one week or longer, up to three weeks.

To make the drinks: In a blender or food processor, put two slices of the rum-soaked pineapple, 1/2 cup of the rum liquid and 1/3 cup coconut milk for each drink. Blend with 2 cups chipped ice carefully, because the pineapple fibers cause this drink to really foam up. Enjoy!

Serves 12

Pepper Rum

Jay loves having this condiment around to add zing to soups or seafood marinades. But it is really good in simple rum drinks, too, because it adds that spark of heat that is the essence of Jamaica!

1/3 cup bird peppers (or chile pequin peppers)
1/3 cup Scotch bonnet peppers
6 ripe pimento (allspice) berries
2 1/2 cups Myers dark rum

Sterilize a stoppered bottle (such as a Grace Jam jar) by washing it with boiling water. Add the peppers, berries, and rum.

Put the top on the bottle, and allow the mixture to stand for several days.

Add a few drops of Pepper Rum to soups or stews to enhance the flavor. If you should start to run low, just add some more rum, and allow the mixture to rest for a couple of days.

Yields 3 cups

Jamaican Shandy

This drink, of British descent, is a perfect thirst quencher. The mixture of beer and ginger beer gives a great effervescent tingle.

1 bottle (12 ounces) Red Stripe beer, chilled
1 bottle (12 ounces) Ginger Beer, chilled
Ice, if desired

Place 2 glasses or mugs in the freezer to chill. When they are frosted, pour half the bottle of beer and half the bottle of ginger beer into each mug. Add ice if you like, and serve immediately.

Serves 2

Granddad's Cure-All

Jay spent a lot of the weekends of his youth on his Uncle Caswell's pimento plantation in Black River. There he saw an awful lot of pimento, the spice the rest of the world calls allspice. His grandfather would often ask him to go to get some ripe pimento berries to make pimento dram.

This rich, spicy "dram" is a traditional in Jamaican home drinks, especially during the Christmas season. The liqueur, made by soaking ripe pimento berries in strong rum, has a rich, spicy character that makes it ideal for sipping straight in cooler climates, or for use in mixed drinks.

Jay's grandfather considered his pimento dram to be a fine medicine. Whenever any of his grandchildren got a cough or cold, out came the Pimento Liqueur, as he liked to call it.

1 quart of ripe pimento berries
1 quart white rum
2 cups lime juice
1 gallon sugar
2 quarts hot water
1/4 pound cinnamon sticks

Put the berries into the rum and lime juice in a nonreactive bowl or crock. Cover the container and allow them to soak for two days.

Stir the sugar into the hot water until the sugar dissolves. Add the cinnamon to the hot syrup. When the syrup is cool, add the rum mixture in which the berries have been steeped. Strain out the seeds, and reserve the liqueur. Store the liqueur in rum bottles or decorative decanters.

Yields about 1 gallon liqueur

Rose Hall

If you don't have a lot of ripe pimento berries around the house, you can still drink pimento dram or use it to make mixed drinks like this one. Several brands of pimento dram are sold in Jamaica; Sangster's Pimento Dram is probably the finest.

1 1/2 ounces pimento dram
1 1/2 ounces orange juice
2 ounces soda or tonic water

Stir the ingredients together well, and serve in a tall ice-filled glass.

Serves 1

Pimento Surprise

Here is another favorite allspice-flavored cocktail.

1/2 ounce Gold Rum 100 proof
1 1/2 ounces pimento dram
2 ounces orange juice
2 ounces pineapple juice
Dash of lime juice
Dash of strawberry syrup

Shake the ingredients well with ice (approximately 1/4 glass). Serve in a cocktail glass.

Serves 1

Fairy Hill Beach

Negril Stinger

The Hedonism resort, once known as Negril Beach Village, is one of the most famous resorts on the island because of its reputation for wild times. At the nude beach is a nude bar, where you can try this Negril special. It's made with Tia Maria, a Jamaican coffee liqueur produced from a recipe that has been closely guarded for generations.

2 ounces Appleton Special Rum or other
    premium light gold rum
1 ounce Tia Maria
1 lime slice, for garnish

Mix the liquid ingredients together, and pour the mixture over a lot of ice in a tall glass. Garnish with the lime slice.

Serves 1

Calico Jack

When Jay was in high school, he took an American girlfriend who was visiting Jamaica to Negril Beach Village (now Hedonism). They arrived late at night and had a couple of Calico Jacks. One thing led to another and they ended up skinny-dipping in the deserted pool. They later discovered, much to their chagrin, that the resort's disco was under the pool, with windows that looked up into the water.

Drink Calico Jacks at your own risk.

1/2 ounce Overproof white rum
1/2 ounce Appleton Special rum
2 ounces pineapple juice
1/2 ounce lime juice
Dash of triple sec
1 pineapple stick and 1 lime slice, for
    garnish

In a bar shaker, blend the first five ingredients well. Pour the mixture over ice cubes or serve it "up," garnished with a pineapple stick and a lime slice.

Serves 1

Pump the Skin

The Grand Lido in Negril is one of Jamaica's plushest luxury resorts. Whether you're sailing aboard its 145-foot restored antique yacht (Aristotle Onassis gave this yacht to Prince Rainier and Princess Grace as a wedding present) or lying on the immaculate beach, a bartender is always close by.

Pump the Skin is one of the special drinks Grand Lido is famous for. A cocktail with pumpkin in it? It tastes better than it sounds; besides, it's very nutritious!

2 2-inch cubes of boiled pumpkin (Big Mama squash)
3 bar spoons granulated sugar
1 ounce evaporated milk
1 ounce white crème de cacao
2 ounces Appleton Gold rum
1 mint sprig and 1 garden cherry (Syrian or Barbados), for garnish

Put the pumpkin, sugar, and liquid ingredients into a blender with 1/4 cup crushed ice. Blend, then pour the mixture into a 10-ounce glass. Garnish with a mint sprig, a garden cherry on a toothpick, and a tall drinking straw.

Serves 1

Red Devil

Almond trees can be found all over the island of Jamaica. When the almonds are ripe, the outer skin turns bright yellow. The skin is sweet and delicious when perfectly ripe, and it makes an unforgettable cocktail. This recipe comes from the Grand Lido.

3 almond skins
1 ounce rum syrup (see page 198)
1/2 ounce lime juice
2 dashes Angostura bitters
1 ounce Appleton Gold rum
1 ounce cherry liqueur
1 thin stalk of sugarcane, 1 pineapple
    slice, and 1 maraschino cherry

Blend the almond skins and the liquid ingredients in a blender with 4 ounces chipped ice. Pour the mixture into a tall glass. Garnish with a thin stick of sugarcane, a pineapple slice, and a cherry.

Serves 1

Breadfruit Boops

If you've never had breadfruit before, you can drink one of these and say you've tried it. This is another invention of the bartenders at Grand Lido.

1 1/2 inch slice boiled breadfruit (2 ounces)
1 ounce Sugar Syrup (see page 52)
2 ounces ginger juice
1 ounce coconut milk
1 ounce crème de banane
1 ounce vodka
1 cinnamon stick and one cherry

Put the breadfruit and the liquid ingredients into a blender with 2 ounces chipped ice. Blend, then pour the mixture into a tall glass. Garnish with a cinnamon stick and a cherry on a toothpick.

Serves 1

Pimento Jam

Here's Grand Lido's version of the allspice-flavored cocktail.

1 ounce pineapple juice
1 ounce apple juice
1 ounce orange juice
1/2 ounce lime juice
1/2 ounce Sugar Syrup (see page 52)
1 1/2 ounce pimento dram
1 ounce Rumona liqueur

1 piece of carrot carved into a ball and
   1 pineapple slice, for garnish

Put the liquid ingredients into a bar shaker with ice cubes. Shake vigorously, then pour into a hollowed pineapple. Garnish with the carrot ball and pineapple slice.

Serves 1

Yellowbird

If you play golf, Tryall Golf and Beach Club is the ultimate Jamaican resort. From the window at the bar, high on a hill, you can watch the action on the impeccably groomed golf course while you sip a Yellowbird. Named after the song by the same name, this mild-flavored but potent drink will definitely put you in a tropical frame of mind.

1 1/4 ounces Gold Label Rum
1/4 ounce apricot brandy
1/4 ounce Liquore Galliano
1/4 ounce fresh lime juice
2 ounces fresh orange juice
1 slice of orange and 1 maraschino
   cherry, for garnish

In a bar shaker, blend the liquid ingredients by shaking well. Pour the mixture over ice in a 10-ounce highball glass. Garnish with the slice of orange and the cherry.

Serves 1

Piña Colada

You'll like this easy piña colada, which is one of Tryall's specialities.

2 ounces coconut milk
1/4 ounce apricot brandy
1/4 ounce light rum
2 ounces pineapple juice
1/4 ounce Sugar Syrup (see page 52)
Pinch of ground cinnamon
Drop of vanilla extract
1 pineapple stick, fresh grated coconut,
   and 1 maraschino cherry, for garnish

Blend the liquid ingredients a the cinnamon in a blender with 3 ounces chipped ice. Serve in a 10-ounce highball glass or hurricane glass, garnished with the pineapple stick, grated coconut, and cherry.

Serves 1

The Astor Hotel's Banana Daiquiri

The Astor Hotel in Mandeville made this version of the banana daiquiri famous. Try it with different varieties of sweet bananas.

1/2 cup Overproof white rum
2 tablespoons confectioners' sugar
Juice of 1 lime
1 ripe banana, sliced
2 1/2 cups chipped ice
2 maraschino cherries

Put the rum, sugar, lime juice, and banana into a blender. With the blender on high speed, slowly add the chipped ice, and blend for 30 seconds.

   Serve the daiquiri in chilled Collins glasses and garnish each glass with a cherry and a straw.

Serves 2

Blue Mountain Cocktail

This drink is claimed by the Blue Mountain Inn, one of the island's most scenic restaurants. The distinguishing flavor in the Blue Mountain Cocktail comes from the coffee liqueur, Tia Maria.

1 1/2 ounces Appleton rum
3/4 ounce vodka
3/4 ounce Tia Maria
2 ounces orange juice
1 ounce lime juice
3 ice cubes

Combine the rum, vodka, Tia Maria, orange juice, and lime juice in a bar shaker. Shake the mixture well with the ice cubes. Pour it into an Old Fashioned glass, and serve.

Serves 1

Blue Nuts

Sangster's Old Jamaica Blue Mountain Coffee Liqueur is an interesting alternative to Tia Maria. It's not quite as sweet, and it has a fuller coffee aroma. Here's one of our favorite recipes from World's End, the Blue Mountain home of Sangster's liqueurs.

2 parts Sangster's Coconut Rum
1 part Sangster's Blue Mountain Coffee
   Liqueur
3 parts milk
Sprinkle of ground pimento (allspice)

Blend the liquid ingredients with 1 part crushed ice. Pour the mixture into a cocktail glass, and sprinkle lightly with the pimento.

Yields whatever amount you desire.

Devon Duppy

Devon House in Kingston is the best-preserved example of colonial architecture in Jamaica. Built in 1881, Devon House was restored by the government and opened to the public in the 1960s. The Grog Shop and the Devonshire Restaurant are two popular gathering places at Devon House where Devon Duppies are served.

Duppy is the Jamaican word for ghost. Like Jamaican duppies, the flavor of this drink of rum, gin, and fresh grapefruit juice will haunt you.

2 ounces Wrey & Nephew rum
1 ounce gin
2 ounces grapefruit juice
1 ounce Sugar Syrup (see page 52)
1/2 ounce lime juice
1 grapefruit twist

Put all the liquid ingredients into a blender, and blend them with 2 ounces crushed ice. Pour the mixture into a tall glass. Garnish with a grapefruit twist, and serve.

Serves 1

Devon House's Ann Bonnie

Named after one of Port Royal's infamous female pirates, this is a ladylike draught of ginger beer with a not-so-ladylike slug of Jamaican rum.

4 ounces ginger beer
2 ounces Appleton Gold rum

Shake the ginger beer and rum together, and serve the drink over ice.

Serves 1

Devon House's Pawpaw

In Jamaica pawpaw means papaya, and Jamaican papaya is the finest anywhere. Especially in this form! This drink has a wonderful pink color.

Chipped ice
1 cup ripe Jamaican pawpaw (papaya), peeled and seeded
1 cup pineapple juice
4 ounces light rum
1/4 cup sugar
Juice of 1 lime

Fill the blender three-quarters full with the ice, then add the other ingredients. Blend the mixture to a slush. Pour it into large cocktail glasses.

Serves 2-4

Old-Style Ginger Beer

Unlike commercial ginger ale, old-fashioned Jamaican ginger beer is supposed to have a bite. This yeast-activated version is creamy and keeps well.

1/2 pound Jamaican gingerroot, grated
   (skin included)
1/2 cup honey
1/2 cup fresh lime juice
4 quarts boiling water
1 cup fresh brewer's yeast
3 cups sugar

Put the ginger and honey into a large bowl, and add the lime juice. Pour all but 1/2 cup of the boiling water over the ginger. Allow the remaining 1/2 cup water to cool a little.

In a small shallow bowl, mix the yeast with 1 cup sugar and the reserved 1/2 cup of warm water, stirring to make a paste. Add the rest of the sugar to the ginger-lime mixture, and stir. Pour the yeast paste into the ginger-lime mixture, and stir again. Cover the bowl with a towel, and let the mixture stand for three days. Skim off the foam, strain the ginger beer and sweeten it to taste. Serve it chilled with spicy foods.

Yields: 1 1/4 gallons

Another Jamaican Ginger Beer

This is a lighter, crisper ginger beer. It has less body than the old-fashioned yeast version, and it doesn't store well, so plan to drink the whole batch quickly.

1 pound Jamaican ginger root, grated
   (skin included)
4 quarts water
1/2 cup lime juice
1 teaspoon vanilla extract
1 ounce Overproof white rum
About 1 pound sugar, to taste

Put the ginger, with the juice that has accumulated, into a large saucepan with 1 quart boiling water. Cover the pan, and turn off the heat. Let the mixture sit until it is cool.

Strain the ginger water twice through a fine wire-mesh strainer to remove the ginger pieces. Discard the pieces in the strainer, and add the lime juice to the remaining ginger water. Pour the mixture into a 5-quart glass container with a lid. Add the remaining 3 quarts water, the vanilla, and the rum (the rum will lose its alcohol over time). Mix well. Stir in the sugar, and chill the ginger beer.

Stir the ginger beer before serving it over ice.

Yields: 4 1/2 quarts

Sister Fire's Guava Juice

For this guava juice—the standard by which to measure all others—you must get 20 perfectly ripe guavas. Sister Fire's "Garden of Eating" had a few trees that were bending over with ripe fruit.

5 cups water
Juice of 3 lemons
1 cup sugar or honey
20 ripe, pink guavas

Pour the water and lemon juice into a large mixing bowl, and add the sugar or honey. Cut the top and bottom off the guavas, and cut them into sixths. Add the guavas to the water, and squeeze with your hands until there are no large pieces of guava left. Let the mixture sit for 15 minutes.

Strain out the seeds with a wire-mesh strainer, forcing as much pulp as possible through the mesh.

Serve the drink over chipped ice.

Serves 8

Sorrel Punch

What Jamaicans call sorrel, or roselle, is a tropical flower—a type of hibiscus, actually—that grows throughout the Caribbean islands. It has a slightly acidic taste and is delicious when mixed with the flavorful island spices and fruits.

Sorrel marks the beginning of the holiday season in Jamaica. Jay's Grandma made the year's first batch of sorrel punch around Thanksgiving, when the first fresh sorrel would show up at the market.

4 cups fresh Jamaican sorrel (or 1/4 cup dried sorrel)
2 cinnamon sticks
4 ounces ginger root, chopped (skin included)
3 cups sugar, honey, or a combination
2 1/2 quarts boiling water
1/2 cup light rum
2 teaspoons ground cinnamon

In a very large crock, combine the sorrel with the cinnamon sticks, ginger, and sugar. Pour the boiling water over all and let the mixture cool. Cover the crock, and let it sit at room temperature for 2 days.

Strain the mixture through a fine sieve or cheesecloth, and return the liquid to the crock. Stir in the rum and cinnamon. Let the mixture stand for 2 more days.

Strain the punch again, and refrigerate it until it is thoroughly chilled.

Serve the punch in chilled glasses filled with crushed ice.

Yields: About 3 quarts

Planter's Punch

1 cup orange juice
1 cup pineapple juice
1 cup grapefruit juice
1 cup strawberry syrup
1 can ginger ale

Mix together all the ingredients except the ginger ale. Chill the mixture.

Add the ginger ale when you are ready to serve the punch. Serve it over chipped or shaved ice.

Serves 6

Mauby Drink

Mauby, sometimes spelled *mawby*, is the bark of a tropical tree. It makes a refreshing drink thought to be very healthful and good for the digestion.

4 ounces mauby bark
2 bay leaves
1 cinnamon stick
9 cups water
1 cup brown sugar

Into a large saucepan, put the mauby bark, bay leaves, and cinnamon. Cover with 8 cups water. Heat the mixture over medium heat until it comes to a boil. Reduce the heat, and let the mixture simmer for 10 to 15 minutes. Let it cool, then strain and chill it.

In a saucepan, combine the brown sugar and the remaining 1 cup water, and heat the mixture over medium heat until the sugar is dissolved. Let the syrup cool, then chill it.

To make a mauby drink, add about 1/4 cup of the brown-sugar syrup to 1/2 cup of the mauby juice. Mix well. Fill a tall 10-to 12-ounce glass with ice. Pour the mixture over the ice, stir well, and serve.

Serves 4

Apsicle

Jamaican resorts are well known for their rum drinks, but the Grand Lido in Negril also pays a lot of attention to their nondrinking guests. This fruity concoction is one of Grand Lido's best nonalcoholic beverages. Angostura bitters give this drink a refreshing edge.

3 ounces apple juice
1 ounce fruit syrup (strawberry or
    orange)
Dash of Angostura bitters
2 ounces ginger beer (see page 67)

Put the liquid ingredients into a bar shaker with 4 ice cubes. Shake vigorously, then pour the liquid into a tall 10 ounce glass. Garnish with an apple slice, and serve.

Serves 1

Sour Mup Mup

Soursop and sweetsop have a creamy consistency that makes this Grand Lido drink very rich and very delicious.

2 chunks pawpaw (papaya)
4 bar spoons soursop
1 small naseberry, peeled
4 bar spoons sweetsop
1/2 ounce coconut milk
1 ounce evaporated milk
2 drops vanilla extract

1 ounce honey
Grated nutmeg and 1 pawpaw slice

Put the fruit and liquid ingredients into a blender with 3 ounces crushed ice. Blend, then pour the drink into a glass. Garnish with grated nutmeg and a pawpaw slice.

Serves 1

Passion Jack

Jackfruit and passion fruit combined with ginger juice make this an exotic Jamaican original. (From Grand Lido)

5 pegs jackfruit, about 3 ounces
2 ounces passion fruit juice
1 ounce Sugar Syrup (see page 52)
1 ounce ginger juice
Dash of lime juice
2 ounces crushed ice
1 thin stick of sugarcane and 1 small
    watermelon slice

Blend the jackfruit and liquid ingredients with the crushed ice until the mixture is smooth. Garnish with a sugarcane stick, a watermelon slice, and a tall straw.

Serves 1

Jamaican Tonics

No discussion of Jamaican beverages would be complete without a mention of Jamaica's favorite folk remedies—tonics. You don't drink a tonic because you're thirsty. You drink it to cure what ails you, improve your love life or calm you down when you can't sleep. Each tonic has a specific purpose.

In Faiths Penn, the Jamaican crossroads that serves up homemade fast food to passing motorists, we noticed a stand with the largest selection of tonics we'd ever seen. At Ragamuffin's Tonic Stand, you just walk up to the window and tell Claudia what your problem is, then she hands you just the tonic you need.

See if you can guess what problem each of these tonics is intended to cure.

Ragamuffin's Tonics:

Disturbance	Okra Slime
Tek Long Fe Come	Magnum
Overdrive	Nightrider
Agony	Irish-Moss
Kick up Rumpus	Pashon Fruit Juice
Mus a fe' Stand Up	

Chapter 3

From Solomon Gundy to Dokono

Appetizers, Lunches, and Snacks

The immense cultural diversity of Jamaican food is reflected not only in its ingredients and flavors but in its etymologies. *Solomon Gundy* is a corruption of the French word and the French dish *salmagundy*. In France, a *salmagundy* or *salmigondis* was an elaborate salad made of many minced ingredients. Originating in the fanciful food era of Louis XIV, the dish has long since gone out of fashion in France. *Dokono*, also called *dunkanoo*, *tie-a-leaf* and *blue drawers*, is an African dish of sweetened starch wrapped up in a banana leaf, a simple preparation that has remained unchanged for centuries. These two dishes represent two vastly different cultures and attitudes about food. But in Jamaica they exist side by side as part of the same cuisine.

In the United States, many ethnic cooking styles have influenced the vast mainstream. In Jamaica there is no mainstream. Jamaican cooking is a patois, a language unto itself, made up of bits and pieces of many other languages.

Nowhere is that patois more colorful than in the everyday foods we call appetizers, lunches, and snacks. Although these sound like dishes of lesser importance, in Jamaica they are, in fact, the runaway favorites. Patties, for instance, are probably the most common food in Kingston, the Jamaican equivalent of Mexico City's taco, New York's hamburger, or London's fish and chips. Crabs, shrimp, and fried fish are favorites everywhere on the island, and they too fall into the category of "appetizers, lunches, and snacks" because they are most often eaten all by themselves.

Enjoy these dishes in that spirit. As preludes to something else, or as little treats that need no more accompaniment than a good appetite and a cold beer.

Solomon Gundy

The word *salmagundy* comes from the Old French words *sal* (salt) and *condir* (to season). True to the spirit of the Old French, this stuff is incredibly salty!

2 pounds pickled shad
1/2 pound pickled mackerel
1/2 pound pickled herring
1 cup cider or malt vinegar
1 tablespoon pimento berries (allspice)
1/2 tablespoon whole black peppercorns
1/4 cup ginger root, chopped
1 cho-cho squash, peeled, seeded, and
    finely diced
1 medium onion, finely chopped (1/2 cup)
4 scallions, finely chopped
1 green Scotch bonnet pepper,
    very finely diced
1 yellow Scotch bonnet pepper,
    very finely diced
1 tablespoon Pickapeppa sauce
1/3 cup peanut or corn oil

Soak all the fish in cold water for at least 4 hours.

Pour off the cold water, and cover the fish with boiling water. Let the fish sit for at least 5 minutes.

Discard the water. Remove all the skin and bones from the fish (needle-nose pliers really help with the bones). Shred the fish as finely as possible.

In a saucepan, boil the vinegar with the allspice, peppercorns, ginger and cho-cho for about 5 minutes. Let it cool.

Mix the shredded fish with the onions, scallions, and Scotch bonnet peppers. Add the Pickapeppa Sauce, and drizzle with the oil. Add the seasoned vinegar and mix well. Let the mixture stand overnight before serving.

Serve Solomon Gundy with crackers. It will keep for weeks in the refrigerator.

Yields 3 cups

Note: Pickled shad, mackerel, and herring unfortunately are not readily available in the United States, so Jay almost always ends up using salted or smoked red herring in place of all the other fish. In a pinch you can use canned sardines as a poor substitute.

Jamaican Stamp 'n Go

Stamp 'n go was originally a sailing term, an order given to seamen meaning "hurry up." Jamaican Stamp 'n Go is a simple codfish fritter. It was an early kind of fast food; travelers would stop at wayside shops to buy one of these ready-made fritters with a slice of bread, and then be on their way. Jay likes to serve them as an appetizer with a salsa or spicy relish such as Gingered Banana Chutney (page 149).

1/4 pound fresh cod (or saltfish [salt cod], soaked in cold water for 1 hour)
Juice of 1 lime
1 medium onion, finely chopped (1/3 cup)
2 tomatoes, finely chopped (1/2 cup)
2 garlic cloves, finely chopped
2 scallions, finely chopped (1/4 cup)
1/4 teaspoon finely diced Scotch bonnet pepper
1 cup flour, sifted
1/2 cup or more very cold water
1 teaspoon paprika
2 tablespoons oil, for frying

Dribble the lime juice over the codfish, pat the fish dry, and dice or finely shred it.

In a skillet, sauté the onions, tomatoes, garlic, scallions, and Scotch bonnet pepper for 3 to 5 minutes, or until the onion is tender.

Put the flour into a large mixing bowl, and stir in cold water till the mixture is the consistency of thick pancake batter. Fold in the cod. Add the sautéed vegetables and paprika.

Heat a heavy skillet or griddle, and add the oil. Ladle batter into the skillet or onto the griddle as you would for pancakes, but spread each fritter thin. Fry the fritters until they are golden brown and crisp on both sides. Drain them on paper towels, and keep them warm until you are ready to serve.

Yields 16 to 20 fritters, depending on your ladle size

Note: Salmon is a good substitute for the codfish, but if you use salmon be sure to add a little salt to the batter. You can add leeks to the batter in addition to the green onions or as a substitute for them. Jay's grandma always used to add 1 teaspoon of baking powder to help "fluff it up."

Pepper Shrimp lady

Middle Quarters Pepper Shrimp

In Middle Quarters, pepper shrimp are sold by the side of the road by the "pepper shrimp ladies." Most of the pepper shrimp in Middle Quarters come from Port Lavaca. You buy the shrimp by the bag—a small bag might contain ten. They are whole freshwater shrimp boiled in their own juices with a lot of salt and fiery hot Scotch bonnet peppers. You had better have a beverage close by when you start eating these.

2 pounds live freshwater shrimp (or crawfish)
6 Scotch bonnet peppers
1/4 cup kosher salt

Place the shrimp, peppers, and salt in a large cast-iron skillet, then heat over an open fire. The shrimp will start to release some o their own water. If you are using crawfish, add 1 cup water to the pan while cooking. Keep stirring until all the shrimps are bright red and firm.

Pepper Shrimp can be eaten hot or cold, but should always be accompanied with a cold Red Stripe.

Serves 3

Jamaican Janga

Janga are crawfish found in the rivers of Jamaica. They have a thinner shell than their Louisiana cousins. In this recipe for pickled janga, you can substitute cooked, peeled, and deveined shrimp.

2 cups cider or malt vinegar
1 Scotch bonnet pepper
1 garlic clove, minced
1 small onion, sliced
4 pimento (allspice) berries, crushed in a
   mortar
1 ounce ginger root, diced (skin included)
Salt and pepper to taste
2 pounds janga (or 1 pound peeled,
   deveined and cooked shrimp)

In a nonreactive saucepan, combine all the ingredients except the janga. Heat the marinate over medium heat until it boils. Put the janga into a heatproof glass dish. Pour the boiling marinade over the janga or shrimp. Cover the dish, let the mixture cool, and store the janga or shrimp in the refrigerator for at least 12 hours before serving.

Serves 4 to 6

Note: Remove the seeds from the Scotch bonnet pepper if you don't want the janga very spicy.

Gut River

One of my favorite excursions when I was a teenager was going down to Gut River. From Mandeville, where I lived, to Gut River is about 13 miles south "as the John crow flies," but thirty-nine miles by car. We always stopped to buy a watermelon on the way.

Gut River is a cold freshwater spring that erupts in a cave about a hundred yards from the warm Caribbean. When we got to Gut River, we would set the watermelon in one of the cold pools and leave it for a few hours to chill. The water was crystal-clear; although the pebbles at the bottom looked like you could pick them up, they were actually 30 feet deep.

As the water flowed down to the beach, it formed chutes or "tunnels" about fifty yards long and full of reeds. We used to swim the whole length in a single breath. Under the reeds, we would find blue crabs by the dozen. We would gather as many as we could and keep them till late in the afternoon to boil. Spring-water boiled crab and naturally chilled watermelon—talk about roughing it!

—Jay McCarthy

Stuffed Blue Crab Backs with Watermelon Salsa

This is as close as you can come to a sunny day on Gut River.

6 to 8 live blue crabs
1 1/2 cups fresh bread crumbs
1 Scotch bonnet pepper, seeded and
    minced
3 tablespoons rum or Pepper Rum
    (see page 55)
2 garlic cloves, crushed
1 ounce gingerroot, grated
1/4 teaspoon ground pimento (allspice)
2 tablespoons chopped cilantro
Zest and juice of 1 lime
Salt to taste
1/4 cup unsalted butter, melted

Preheat the oven to 350 degrees. Cook the crabs in a large pot of salted boiling water for 10 minutes. Let them cool, then remove the meat from the shell and the claws. Try to keep the meat in as big pieces as possible. Scrub the shells thoroughly and reserve them.

In a bowl, combine the crab meat and 1 cup of the bread crumbs, folding them gently together. Add the pepper, rum, garlic, gingerroot, pimento, cilantro, lime zest and juice, and salt. Mix well. Stuff the crab shells with the mixture, sprinkle over the remaining 1/2 cup of bread crumbs, and drizzle with the melted butter. Place the stuffed shells on a baking pan, and bake for 30 minutes. Serve the crabs hot with Watermelon Salsa (see page 150).

Serves 6 to 8

Smoked Marlin

Marlin meat is similar to swordfish in color and size, but it has a slightly larger grainy texture. Smoking enhances its grainy character and keeps it from drying out too much.

1 gallon Basic Brine (see below)
4 pounds marlin loin, or center cut
1/2 pound "sweet" wood chips, such as pecan, apple, cherry, pimento or peach, for smoking

Put the brine and marlin into a nonreactive container. To be sure the fish is covered with liquid, use a plate to keep it submerged. Let the marlin cure in the refrigerator or packed in ice for 2 to 4 hours.

To smoke the marlin, fire up your smoker or grill. When the coals are white, add the wood chips. Smoke the fish on top of ice—in an ice-filled pan, or on commercial or homemade ice packs. The idea is to keep the fish cold while smoking it. Smoke for an hour, or until the marlin is firm to touch. If the marlin needs to cook longer, bake it at 350° for 20 to 30 minutes.

Chill the fish. When it is thoroughly chilled, slice it thinly for a salad, or flake it into large pieces for a pepperpot soup (see page 107).

Serves 8 to 10

Basic Brine

Jay uses this brine for almost anything he smokes. The more dense the food is, the longer it should cure. When using a liquid cure, always keep the food refrigerated or chilled during the curing-brining process.

1 1/2 cups kosher or coarse sea salt
1 cup brown sugar
1 gallon water
2 tablespoons red pepper flakes
1/4 cup chopped ginger root (skin included)

12 pimento (allspice) berries
12 coriander seeds

In a 2-gallon nonreactive container, dissolve the salt and brown sugar in the water. Add the remaining spices.

Yields 1 gallon

Pickapeppa's Peppa-Q-Shrimp

The only bad thing about this recipe is that it uses a whole bottle of Pickapeppa sauce, so afterward you have to go buy a new one.

2 pounds fresh jumbo shrimp, with shells
    and heads, if possible
1/2 cup olive oil
5 garlic cloves, thinly sliced
1 tablespoon coarse-ground black pepper
1 teaspoon kosher or coarse sea salt
1 1/2 teaspoon dried rosemary, crushed
1 bottle Pickapeppa Sauce
Juice of 2 lemons
1/4 pound unsalted butter, cut into
    thin squares
1/2 cup beer, at room temperature (Red
    Stripe is just fine)

Place the shrimp in a 9 x 12 ovenproof glass dish. Pour the olive oil over the shrimp, to partially cover it. Scatter the garlic slices over the shrimp, and sprinkle generously with the pepper, salt, and rosemary. Cover all the shrimp with Pickapeppa Sauce, then drizzle with the lemon juice. Marinate the shrimp for approximately 2 hours at room temperature, shaking the dish occasionally.

Preheat the oven to 350 degrees. Cover the dish with the beer and squares of butter. Bake the shrimp for 10 minutes, rearranging or turning them during the cooking, if necessary, so they cook evenly. They are done when the shells turn red and you can see a space between the meat and the shell.

Serve the shrimp immediately, with plenty of hot French bread to soak up the sauce.

Serves 4

Note: If you'd like the sauce thicker, remove the baked shrimp, then simmer the sauce on the stove top till the desired consistency is achieved.

Land Crabs

These crabs live in holes on dry ground. After a rain sometimes, they are flooded out of their holes, and it's easy to catch sackfuls of them.

3 gallons boiling water
4 large onions, chopped
1 garlic head, split in half horizontally
1 tablespoon pimento (allspice) berries
1 tablespoon whole black peppercorns
6 to 8 thyme sprigs
2 to 3 whole Scotch bonnet peppers
Salt to taste
6 to 8 live land crabs, in a sack

Bring the water to a boil in a large pot with a tight-fitting lid. Add the remaining ingredients, and simmer for a couple of minutes. Pour the crabs out of the sack into the pot, and boil them for 15 minutes.

Drain, then serve the crabs in the shell, or use the meat in a salad or appetizer.

Serves 4

Shark Bites

Shark meat has a tendency to get tough rather quickly and consequently needs a little extra attention. These Shark Bites make a great party snack.

4 pounds mako shark
4 cups Wet Jerk Rub (see page 118)
1 cup soy sauce
1 cup mango or pawpaw (papaya) purée
Salt and pepper to taste

Cut the shark fillets across the grain about 1/4 inch thick (thick enough to insert a bamboo skewer through lengthwise). Mix together the jerk seasoning, soy sauce, and mango purée. Toss the shark strips in the marinade. Remove the strips one at a time, skewer them lengthwise, and set the skewers aside.

Shark is best cooked on a griddle, but it can be grilled; just be careful not to burn the skewers. Cook the shark just until the meat is pearly white (shark does not retain moisture well, and overcooking it even a little makes it tough). Add salt and pepper to taste.

Arrange the skewers decoratively on a platter, and serve them with spicy salsa.

Serves 8 to 10

Traditional Patties

Patty (1870)—a semicircular pastry made by folding a circle of pastry upon itself over a filling of ground meat, plantains, fruit paste, or the like. Also called a tart when made with fruit. Plantain patties are very popular in St. Andrew.
—The Dictionary of Jamaican English

Patties are as essential to the Jamaican way of life as rum, jerk, and going to market. They are eaten almost as frequently as hamburgers are in the United States. Patties are rarely made at home; people buy them from patty vendors, by the dozen or individually. Patties can be bought frozen, but those fresh out of the oven can't be beat.

Everybody has their own favorite patty shop of the moment. The thing that most distinguishes the patties made by different vendors is the crust. The perfect patty crust is light and flaky, never pasty.

The traditional patty filling is made with beef. Devon House, however, is famous for its curried chicken and shrimp patties; a new chain called Mother's is making a name for itself with vegetable and callaloo patties; and resorts on the north coast even make lobster patties.

If you haven't got a patty shop in your neighborhood, here's a recipe for making them at home.

Patty Pastry

4 cups flour
1/2 teaspoon baking powder
2 teaspoons ground turmeric
1 teaspoon salt
1 cup vegetable shortening, at room temperature
1 cup very cold water

Traditional Patty Filling

1 1/2 pounds ground beef or pork
2 onions, finely chopped
5 scallions, finely chopped
2 to 3 Scotch bonnet peppers, finely chopped
2 tablespoons fresh thyme leaves, chopped
2 garlic cloves
1 tablespoon ginger root, grated
2 tablespoons vegetable oil
5 cups (3/4 pound) fresh bread crumbs
3/4 teaspoon turmeric or Jamaican curry powder
Salt and pepper to taste
3/4 cup water

To make the pastry dough, sift together the flour, baking powder, turmeric, and salt. Cut in the shortening with a pastry blender or two knives until the dough has the consistency of coarse cornmeal. While mixing in an electric mixer with a dough hook or by hand with a fork, slowly add cold water just till the dough holds together. For a light crust avoid overworking the dough. Wrap the dough in foil or plastic, and chill it while you make the filling. (You can refrigerate the dough as long as overnight, but remember to let it warm up a little before using it.)

To make the filling, put the beef or pork into a bowl, and add the onions, scallions, Scotch bonnet peppers, thyme, garlic, and ginger. Mix well. Heat the oil in a "dutchy" (dutch oven) or large skillet, and cook the meat over medium high heat until it is lightly browned, about 10 minutes. Add the bread crumbs, turmeric, salt, and pepper, and stir well. Add the water, cover the pan, and simmer the mixture for 30 minutes. The mixture should be the consistency of thick chili—wet, not runny or dry and crumbly. Allow the filling to cool while you roll out the pastry.

Preheat the oven to 400 degrees. To assemble the patties, divide the dough into 24 equal pieces. On a lightly floured surface, roll out each piece of dough to the thickness of a pencil (1/4 inch). Using a small soup bowl or a 4-inch round cookie cutter, cut the dough into a circle. Keep the patty dough circles moist by stacking them and covering them with a damp cloth. After all the circles are cut, spoon enough filling into the center of each circle to cover half of it. Fold the pastry circle in half, and crimp the edge with a fork. Bake the patties on an ungreased baking sheet for 30 to 35 minutes. Serve them hot. Freeze the leftovers for a quick snack later on.

Serves 12

Note: If you don't have turmeric, you can substitute curry powder or 'natta or ground annatto (achiote) in the pastry dough. Suet, lard, butter, or a combination of these, in place of the vegetable shortening, adds extra richness to the crust.

Curry Shrimp, Chicken, or Vegetable Patties

4 scallions, finely chopped
2 Scotch bonnet peppers
1/2 1-pound loaf french bread, broken
    into large pieces
8 thyme sprigs, leaves only
1 1/2 pounds shrimp, peeled, deveined,
    and boiled; or 1 1/2 pounds boiled
    chicken meat; or 6 cups cooked
    mixed vegetables such as carrots,
    cho-chos, celery, callaloo, potatoes,
    green banana
2 garlic cloves, chopped fine
1 tablespoon ginger root, grated
3/4 teaspoon Jamaican curry powder
1 teaspoon salt
1 to 2 teaspoons Annatto Oil (see page
    154) or about 1 teaspoon paprika
24 patty pastry circles (see page 88)

In a food processor, grind the scallions and the peppers together. Set the mixture aside.

Put the bread into a large saucepan, and pour enough cold water over it to cover it. Let it soak for a few minutes, then squeeze the bread dry, saving the water. Pass the bread through a food mill, and return the ground bread to the reserved water. Add the thyme leaves, and cook the bread over medium heat, stirring occasionally, till it is quite dry. Combine the shrimp, or the chicken, or the vegetables, and the scallions and peppers, with the cooked bread. Add the garlic, ginger, curry, and salt and enough annatto oil or paprika to color the filling. Cook the mixture over medium heat, stirring occasionally, for 10 more minutes. Remove the pan from the heat, and let the mixture cool.

Assemble and bake the patties as directed on page 89. Serve them hot.

Serves 12

Dokono

Still eaten by the African tribes to which Jamaica's blacks trace their ancestry, Jamaican dokono has been adapted to the sources of starch indigenous to different parts of the island. In Port Antonio, dokono might be made with bananas and grated coconut. In St. Thomas, it is made with plantains; in St. Elizabeth, cassava or corn is used. In Westmoreland, you can find dokono filled with potatoes. In some parishes, sweet potatoes are a key element, and in a lot of places the "pudding" is sweetened with sugar.

Dokono tastes best steamed like Mexican tamales, although sometimes the packets are boiled or even roasted. Adding corncobs to the boiling water gives a much better corn flavor, whether you steam or boil the dokono.

6 nearly dry ears of corn, grated, or 3
    cups coarse cornmeal
1 cup brown sugar
2 cups coconut cream
1/2 cup raisins
2 teaspoons ground cinnamon
1/4 teaspoon ground ginger
24 6" x 6" pieces of banana leaf

Grate the corn into a medium bowl. Add the remaining ingredients except the leaves, and stir the mixture to a paste.

Bring a large pot of water to a boil over medium heat. "Quail" (as they say in Jamaica) the banana leaf pieces by dipping them into the boiling water or heating them over an open flame to make them pliable. Place 2 tablespoons of the dokono mixture on each banana leaf, fold the leaf into a packet, and tie the packet with a long piece of banana leaf or string. Drop the dokono packets into the boiling water, and simmer them over low heat for about 45 minutes. When the packets are done, they should feel firm.

Remove the packets from the water, allow them to cool, and serve.

Yields 24 dokono

Callaloo Rundown on Fried Plantains

Robb sampled these little plantain rounds topped with spicy callaloo at Tryall Golf, Tennis and Beach Club, and he couldn't stop eating them.

3 cups coconut milk
1 thyme sprig
1/2 cup onion, diced
1/2 cup tomato, diced
6 scallions, chopped
1 Scotch bonnet pepper, seeded and
    chopped
2 pounds callaloo or spinach, stemmed
    and coarsely chopped
Salt and pepper to taste
1/4 cup vegetable oil
4 ripe plantains, peeled, sliced into
    1/2-inch-thick rounds

In a saucepan, bring the coconut milk to a boil. Boil it, stirring constantly, until it is reduced by half. Add the thyme, onion, tomatoes, scallions, Scotch bonnet pepper, and callaloo. Cook the mixture for 8 minutes, or until it is thick. Season it with salt and pepper.

In a large skillet, heat the oil. Fry the plantain slices, in batches, until they are golden brown. Drain them.

Put a little of the callaloo mixture on top of each plantain round. Bake the rounds with their topping for 10 minutes. Serve them hot.

Yields 48 pieces

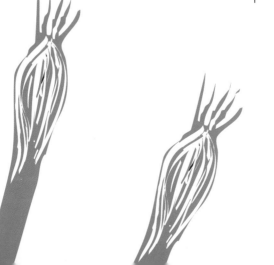

Fried Ackee Morsels

Don't give up on ackee just because you're not crazy about ackee and saltfish. Here's an ackee recipe everybody loves.

12 ackees
3 cups water, salted
1/4 cup unsalted butter
1/4 cup Cinnamon-Thyme Oil
    (see page 155)
6 scallions
Salt and pepper to taste

Prepare the ackees by discarding the seeds and removing the pink skin. Place the ackees in a saucepan, cover them with the salted water, and simmer them for 5 minutes over low heat. Drain the ackees.

In a heavy skillet, heat the butter. Add the ackees and the scallions, and sauté for 3 to 5 minutes or until soft.

Season with salt and pepper. Drain on paper towels. Toss with the cinnamon oil, then arrange the ackees decoratively on a plate. Serve them with a tomato relish or mango chutney.

Serves 12

Scotch Bonnet Olives

Jay created these olives because he loves the Scotch bonnet pepper as much as he loves olives. Jay was really thinking of putting them in Stoli martinis, but the cooks in his restaurant ate them all before the olives made it to the bar. Now Jay just keeps them in the kitchen and occasionally tosses them in with a pasta dish.

1 gallon large Spanish Imperial pickled
    green olives, drained and rinsed
3 cups cider vinegar
4 to 6 ounces gingerroot, coarsely
chopped into 1-inch pieces
2 onions, cut into crescents lengthwise
6 to 10 whole Scotch bonnet peppers
2 stalks lemongrass
12 pimento (allspice) berries
12 whole black peppercorns
24 coriander seeds
6 bay leaves
1/2 cup sugar

Pour the olives out of the glass jar into a strainer, and rinse the brine off them. Rinse the jar and lid first with cold water, then with boiling water.

    In a saucepan, heat the vinegar with the remaining ingredients, simmer for about 10 minutes. Let the vinegar cool completely, then pour it into the olive jar. Return the olives to the jar, and refrigerate them for at least a week. They will keep for several months in the refrigerator.

Yields 150 olives

Pickled Cho-Cho

2 cucumbers, seeded, cut in half
    and sliced into crescents
2 cho-cho, peeled and cut into crescents
2 red onions, thinly sliced into crescents
1 tablespoon pimento (allspice) berries
1 cup cider vinegar
2 whole Scotch bonnet peppers
1 teaspoon salt
1/2 tablespoon coriander seeds
1/4 cup julienne carrots

1/2 tablespoon cracked pepper
1/4 cup julienned unpeeled ginger root

Put all the ingredients into a nonreactive saucepan, and bring to a boil. Simmer for 5 minutes, then remove the pan from the heat. Let the pickles cool. Refrigerate. Serve the pickles with escoveitch (page 136).

Yields 2 cups

Pickled Pumpkin

You'll sometimes see a squash in American supermarkets called a Big Mama. It is very similar in color and taste to Jamaican pumpkin.

1 5- to 6-pound pumpkin, (Big Mama squash) peeled and cut into 1-inch cubes (about 4 quarts)
4 to 5 cups sugar
4 cups cider or cane vinegar
3 cups water
2 cinnamon sticks
2 ounces gingerroot, cut into 1/2-inch pieces
1 tablespoon pimento (allspice) berries
1 1/2 teaspoons whole cloves
2 cups orange juice, fresh (or 6 ounces frozen concentrate) without water

Wash and rinse 8 or 9 pint canning jars and lids, and keep them hot.

In a large nonreactive pot, combine the sugar, vinegar, water, and spices (tie the spices in cheesecloth, if you prefer). Heat the mixture over high heat until it is boiling, stirring constantly. Continue to heat and stir until all the sugar is dissolved. Stir in the squash chunks and orange juice, and return to a boil. Reduce the heat, and simmer the squash, stirring occasionally, until it is barely tender, about 30 minutes.

Ladle the squash and liquid into the hot jars to 1/2 inch from the top, covering the squash with hot liquid. Wipe the tops and threads of the jars with a damp cloth. Put on the lids, and screw on the bands. Process the jars in a boiling water bath for 5 minutes. Let the jars cool undisturbed for 12 to 24 hours.

Check the lids; they should be depressed and inflexible. If they are not, reheat the ingredients and reseal the jars. Label the jars, and store them in a cool, dark place. Before using the pickles check for signs of spoilage. Do not keep the pickles longer than a year.

Yields 8 to 9 pints, if the squash is cut in 1-inch cubes.

Fairy Hill Beach

Chapter 4

Teas, Waters, and Pepperpots

Jamaica's Favorite Soups

Soup is big in Jamaica. Whether it's in the form of fish tea, mannish water, or pepperpot, soup is one of the most popular dishes on the island. In fact, pepperpot was one of the original foods of Jamaica, tracing its history all the way back to the Arawak Indians.

Like chicken soup in American Jewish culture, Jamaican soups are regularly used as a sort of folk medicine. Cow-cod soup and mannish water enjoy a reputation for being able to restore or enhance a man's virility. Every groom in Jamaica eats mannish water on his wedding night—if he knows what's good for him.

Soups aren't often eaten as a course before an entrée; they are more likely to be dinner itself. They are especially hearty with the addition of "spinners," "pot bellies," or any of the other "serious dumplings" that Jamaicans love to put in their soup.

Try one of these hearty Jamaican soups for dinner; they're bound to cure what ails ya.

Fish Tea

This may not taste like any "tea" you've ever had before. Tea is synonymous with broth in Jamaica; the term is a leftover from the days of British rule. The clear soups called teas are popular for lunch, light dinners, and late-night snacks. They are sometimes strained and drunk as a beverage.

5 pounds fresh fish (preferably snapper, kingfish, or parrotfish)
5 whole black peppercorns
2 pimento (allspice) or bay leaves
6 thyme sprigs
3 to 4 potatoes, peeled and cut into 1-inch cubes
1 dozen green bananas, peeled and cut into 1-inch lengths
2 cho-cho squashes, peeled and cut into 1/2-inch cubes
4 scallions, finely chopped
1 Scotch bonnet pepper, whole
Juice of 2 limes
1/2 teaspoon salt
2 onions, finely chopped

Put the fish in the pot, and cover it with water. Season with the peppercorns, pimento or bay leaves, and 3 thyme sprigs. Simmer the fish 30 minutes, covered.

Strain the stock, and pick the fish from the bones. Discard the bones, and return the fish meat to the stock. Add the potatoes, green bananas, cho-cho, scallions, Scotch bonnet pepper, onions and remaining 3 sprigs thyme. Simmer the soup, covered, for 30 to 40 minutes, until the banana and potatoes are tender. Add lime juice and salt to taste.

Serves 10 to12

Jamaican Red-Pea Soup

When Jay was young and lived with his family in New York, their Jamaican housekeeper, Miss Lou, used to make this thick pea soup for the children. On a cold day, they felt warm and loved inside out after having a bowl of this soup. Miss Lou used to complain about having to use new potatoes instead of Jamaican dasheen.

1 1/2 pounds beef stew meat
3/4 pound pig's tail
2 cups red peas (kidney beans), picked
    over and rinsed
4 quarts water
1/2 pound dasheen
3 scallions
3 thyme sprigs
1 whole green Scotch bonnet pepper
Salt to taste

Put the stew meat, pig's tail, and peas into the water in a large pot. Bring the ingredients to a boil, cover the pot, and boil until the peas are nearly cooked, about 20 minutes. Then add the dasheen, scallions, thyme, Scotch bonnet pepper, and salt. Boil until the peas are completely cooked, and then remove and discard the Scotch bonnet pepper. Remove the meat, and set it aside. Pass the soup through a colander or food mill, discarding the pea skins. Taste the soup for flavor and consistency, return the meat to the pot, and add salt, water, or both to suit your taste.

Serve the soup hot.

Serves 4 to 6

Pumpkin Soup

The best pumpkin soup we sampled was served on the patio of Kingston's Devonshire restaurant late one night. Here's the traditional recipe for this old favorite. Spinner dumplings turn this soup into a meal (see page 102).

1 onion, finely diced
2 pounds pumpkin (Big Mama squash), diced large
2 quarts water
1 whole Scotch bonnet pepper
2 scallions, finely chopped
2 garlic cloves, crushed
4 thyme sprigs
2 marjoram sprigs
2 bay leaves
Pinch each of white pepper and salt

In a large soup pot, sweat the onions (heat without oil or added water) over medium heat until they are translucent. Add the pumpkin, water, and whole pepper. Bring the ingredients to a simmer, and add the remaining ingredients. Simmer the soup to the desired consistency, about 30 to 35 minutes.

Unless you enjoy very spicy soup, remove the pepper. Serve the soup hot.

Basic Dumplings

This recipe makes what are called "heavy" or, if made very round, "pot belly" dumplings. You can use the same recipe to make about four dough-nut-shaped "serious" dumplings.

Jay's mother is something of a dumpling connoisseur. She hates what she calls "dense dumplings," so she adds about 1 teaspoon baking powder to her dumpling dough to make them light. Jay uses club soda instead of water to get the same "light and fluffy" effect.

1 cup flour
1/4 teaspoon salt
About 1/3 cup club soda

Sift the flour and salt into a bowl, and slowly stir in enough club soda to make a stiff dough (a sticky dough makes a mushy dumpling). Knead the dough in the bowl or on a lightly floured surface until it is smooth. Shape it into eight small balls that each fit in the palm of your hand.

Drop the dumplings into boiling salted water, and cook them for 15 to 20 minutes. Or add them to soups and stews, and cook them for as long or longer.

Serve the dumplings in soup or as a side dish.

Yields 8 dumplings

Note: When Jay makes dumplings at his restaurant, he often adds fresh herbs to the dough to complement the soup or stew they are to be used in. Some pleasant additions are fresh thyme, cilantro, ginger, and even coconut.

Soup Dumplings

There are many nicknames for dumplings in Jamaica, each indicating a style of preparation. Jay grew up with spinners (rolled between the hands into strands), pot bellies (rounded in the palm), heavies (large dumplings), and serious dumplings (doughnut-shaped). There are other kinds, too, such as little johnny (a small finger-shaped dumpling) and man-to-man (they go straight to the stomach). Even johnny cakes are sometimes referred to as "breakfast dumplings."

Cornmeal Dumplings

1 cup flour
3/4 cup cornmeal
1 teaspoon baking powder
1 teaspoon salt
3 scallions, finely chopped
3 tablespoons cold vegetable shortening
    or unsalted butter
1/3 cup very cold water

Into a mixing bowl, put the flour, cornmeal, baking powder, salt and scallions. With a pastry cutter or two knives, cut in the shortening until the mixture resembles coarse cornmeal. Stir in the cold water to make a stiff dough. Roll the dough into 24 balls.

Bring a large pot of salted water to a boil. Drop in the dumplings, cover the pan, and simmer the dumplings for 10 to 15 minutes, until the dumplings are done; or add the dumplings to a stew or pepperpot, and cook them the same way.

Yields 24 dumplings

Beefy Banana Soup

In Jamaica, green bananas are eaten as a vegetable. They are not at all sweet, but have a mild starchy flavor.

1 large (5- to- 6 pound) beef bone, or 2
   pounds beef stew meat (or both)
1 gallon water or beef stock
2 bay leaves
8 whole black peppercorns
3 pimento (allspice) berries
14 green bananas, peeled and split
   lengthwise
4 new potatoes, quartered
2 vine-ripened tomatoes (about
   1 pound), diced
4 scallions
2 garlic cloves, minced
Liquid from 4 coconuts, or about 2 cups
   coconut milk
6 thyme sprigs
1 teaspoon salt, or to taste
1 teaspoon ground black pepper, or
   to taste

Put the beef bone and/or meat into the water or stock. Add the bay leaves, peppercorns, and pimento. Simmer for 4 hours.

Drop the bananas into a large pot of boiling salted water. Simmer them, uncovered, for 15 to 20 minutes. Remove the bananas, dice them, and set them aside.

Add the potatoes, tomatoes, scallions, and garlic to the beef stock, which should be approximately 3/4 gallon. Over high heat, reduce the stock by half. This should take about 30 to 45 minutes.

Add the diced bananas to the soup. Add the coconut milk, thyme, salt, and pepper. Cook the soup for 5 more minutes, and then serve it hot.

Serves 10

Note: If you like, spice this soup up with Pickapeppa or another Jamaican hot sauce. This soup is also good with dumplings.

Pepperpot

Cassareep is a major flavoring agent in the original version of this savory stew. The juice of the boiled-down grated cassava, flavored with brown sugar, cinnamon, cloves, and other ingredients, cassareep is one of the oldest condiments in the Caribbean. Its origins can be traced back to the Arawak Indians; it was discussed in chronicles that date back to Columbus's time. (In their raw form, cassava and the juice of the cassava are highly poisonous.)

Jay's Aunt Shirley told him that some of his family back in the old country home of St. Elizabeth used byne spear in their pepperpot. The young bud of the night-blooming cereus, byne spear has the consistency of a large okra pod. Byne pear, the flower bud of either a type of climbing cactus or a prickly pear, can be used the same way. Jay's Aunt Shirley went to the trouble of collecting a byne spear for us to use in testing her pepperpot recipe.

Aunt Cassie's Jamaican Pepperpot Soup

Dear Aunt Cassie says Aunt Shirley can use all the byne spear she wants in her soup, but Aunt Cassie is not climbing any trees to look for any! Jay's Aunt Cassie gave him this recipe many years ago, and it always takes him back to his grandmother's kitchen. It also reminds him of the "Great Dumpling Debate." It seems everyone in the family prefers a different kind of dumpling, but they always make the ones his mother likes because she makes the most noise about it.

1 1/2 pounds beef stew meat
3/4 pound pig's tail
About 4 quarts water
1/2 pound dasheen, 1/4-inch diced
2 1/2 pounds fresh spinach, finely
    chopped
1 1/2 pounds kale or callaloo, finely
    chopped
12 fresh okra pods, cut into small rings
1 hard-boiled egg
1 whole green Scotch bonnet pepper
1 medium onion, finely chopped
2 garlic cloves, crushed and minced
3 scallions
4 thyme sprigs
1/2 cup coconut milk
Salt and pepper to taste

Put the stew meat and the pig's tail into a large soup pot and cover them with water. Bring the mixture to a boil. Boil until the meat is nearly completely cooked, then add the dasheen. Put the spinach, callaloo, and okra into a saucepan with a little water. Cover the pan, and cook the greens, over medium heat, for about 8 minutes. Rub the steamed greens through a colander or food mill into the soup kettle. Add the egg and the Scotch bonnet pepper, onion, garlic, scallions, and thyme. Simmer the soup until it thickens, then add the coconut milk. Simmer the soup for 5 minutes more. Season it with salt and pepper, and serve.

Serves 10

Note: Byne spear, if available, can be substituted for the okra in the above recipe.

Uncle Michael's Oxtail Pepperpot

Jay's Uncle Michael James raised cattle in Black River. He always saved the best oxtails for his own version of pepperpot.

1 pound oxtails
2 onions, minced
1/2 cup minced scallions
6 thyme sprigs
6 pimento (allspice) berries
3 garlic cloves, crushed and minced
Salt and pepper to taste
1 pound pork, cut into 1-inch cubes
2 tablespoons vegetable oil
1 pound dasheen or yellow yam, peeled
    and diced to 1/2-inch

If your oxtails are salted, soak them for an hour or two in cold water. Discard the water.

In a bowl, combine the onions, scallions, thyme, allspice, garlic, and salt and pepper. Rub this mixture into the oxtails and pork. Allow the meat to marinate in a pot in the refrigerator for at least 1 hour, or overnight.

Heat a cast-iron pot. Add the oil, and brown the meat well. Add a little water only if necessary; the meat should brown in its own fat. Cover the pot, and cook the meat over low heat for several hours, until the meat is very tender. Add the dasheen or yam about an hour before the meat is done.

Although Uncle Michael never put dumplings in this oxtail stew, you may like to add them, as we do.

Serves 4 to 6

Smoked Marlin Pepperpot

In some of the earliest references to pepperpot soup, all sorts of ingredients were mentioned, including bamboo shoots, cotton tree tips, and prawns and crawfish. So, while Jay's original recipe that follows may seem unique, he says it is not really all that innovative to include fresh or smoked marlin in a pepperpot.

4 quarts water
2 1/2 pounds spinach, finely chopped
1 pound fresh okra, chopped
1 1/2 pound kale or callaloo, finely
    chopped
2 cho-cho squashes, peeled and grated
1/2 pound dasheen, 1/4-inch diced
1 medium onion, finely chopped
2 garlic cloves, crushed and minced
1 ounce grated gingerroot
3 scallions, chopped
4 thyme sprigs
2 bay leaves
1 whole green Scotch bonnet pepper
1/2 cup coconut milk
2 pounds fresh or smoked marlin
    (see page 84), flaked
Salt and pepper to taste

Bring the water and the first nine ingredients to a boil in a large soup pot. Cover the pot, and simmer for 15 to 20 minutes. Pass the mixture through a colander or food mill, then return it to the pot. Add the thyme, bay leaves, and Scotch bonnet pepper. Simmer until the soup thickens, then add the coconut milk and the marlin. Simmer 5 minutes more, season with salt and pepper, and serve.

Serves 10

Cow-Cod Soup

Cow-cod soup is supposed to make men virile. But then again, so is mannish water, and so is peanut-root tonic. All over the island, recipes can be found for restoratives, tonics, and all-purpose aphrodisiacs. Cow-cod soup is one of these recipes. When we tried this version at Faiths Pen, a couple of the local vendors gave us big Jamaican smiles with that universal twinkle in their eyes.

3 quarts salted water
1 cow cod (testicles), deveined, connec-
    tive tissue removed, and minced
1/2 Scotch bonnet peppers, minced
1 medium onion, diced
1 celery stalk, diced
1 dasheen, peeled and diced
1 cup pumpkin (Big Mama squash),
    peeled and diced

2 thyme sprigs
4 pimento (allspice) berries
1/2 tablespoon arrowroot
Juice of 1 lime
Dash of freshly grated nutmeg

Put the salted water into a large pot, and bring the water to a boil. Add the cleaned cow cod. Bring the water to a second boil, skim off the scum, and add the Scotch bonnet pepper. Lower the heat, and simmer the cow cod gently for 6 to 7 hours.

Take the cow cod out of the pot, cut it into bite-size pieces, and return it to the pot. Add the vegetables, thyme, allspice, and arrowroot. Bring the soup to a boil again, then lower the heat, and cook till the vegetables are done, about 30 minutes.

Add the lime juice and nutmeg just before serving.

Serves 8 to 10

Mannish Water

If a Jamaican calls you "mannish," the person means you are forward or impertinent. Mannish water is a bold, forthright stew made from the head of a goat with a lot of dumplings added. It makes you "mannish" as in *macho*. It is always served to grooms on their wedding nights, and it's also popular for other festive occasions. The best mannish waters seem to be the ones that cook all day in a 5-gallon coconut oil tin on top of three stones, over an open fire near the beach.

4 quarts water (or enough to cover the goat's head)
2 pounds goat's head, feet, or both
2 pounds goat stew meat
2 small onions, chopped
2 garlic cloves, minced
10 pimento (allspice) berries
10 whole black peppercorns
3 bay leaves
1/2 tablespoon salt
1/2 cup vegetable oil
4 carrots, diced
2 dasheens, peeled and cubed
2 pounds potatoes, peeled and cubed
1/4 pound pumpkin (Big Mama squash), peeled and cubed
6 green bananas, peeled
5 scallions, finely chopped
2 to 3 whole Scotch bonnet peppers
2 cups Jamaican Overproof white rum

In a large, heavy pot, combine the water, goat's head, goat meat, onions, garlic, pimento, peppercorns, bay leaves, and salt. Bring the mixture to a rolling boil, and skim off any scum. Cover the pot, and, over medium heat, cook for 30 minutes, or until the meat falls off the bone.

Sauté the carrots, dasheen, potatoes, pumpkin, green bananas, scallions, and peppers in the oil for 3 to 5 minutes, then add to the stew. Cook the stew at least an hour—2 or 3 hours is better—and then add the rum. Cook one hour more before serving.

Serves 10 to 12

Note: We heard a lot of discussion about whether to add banana peel to the soup. Apparently, adding finely chopped banana peel makes the soup extra "mannish."

Shrimp Stock

This simple stock adds great flavor to many seafood dishes. Use it for cooking the rice to accompany any seafood entrée or for outstanding depth of flavor in soups and chowders.

2 pounds shrimp heads, shells, or both
1 medium onion, quartered
1 garlic clove
1 celery rib
1 carrot, chopped
1/2 cup white wine

Preheat the oven to 350 degrees. Spread the shrimp heads and shells in a baking pan, and roast them until the shells are red and all the liquid has evaporated.

Sweat the onion, garlic, celery and carrot in a large pot. Add the shrimp heads and shells, and cover with cold water (it's important that the water be cold). Bring the water and shrimp heads and shells to a boil. Pour the white wine into the pan in which the shrimp heads and shells were roasted, and scrape the bottom of the pan. Add the wine and scrapings to the stock.

Simmer the stock for at least 1 hour, uncovered, adding liquid if the level in the pot falls below 1 quart. Strain the stock, and reserve it.

Yields 1 quart.

Land Crab Soup

The water in which land crabs are cooked cannot be used for soup because it is so dirty. Use a stock made from shrimp shells and heads (see page 110), if you can get them. In this recipe other flavors, including ginger, lemongrass (called fevergrass in Jamaica) and coconut are infused into the stock while it reduces.

1/4 cup vegetable oil
8 carrots, peeled and chopped
2 onions, chopped
1/2 cup tomato paste
1/4 cup flour
4 stalks lemongrass
1 cup coconut milk
3 ounces ginger root
6 pimento (allspice) berries
6 thyme sprigs
1 whole Scotch bonnet pepper
2 gallons Shrimp Stock (see page 110)
2 cups heavy cream
1 pound land crab or other crab meat

In a large pot, heat the oil. Sauté the carrots and the onions till the onions are translucent. Stir in the tomato paste. Sprinkle the carrots and onions with the flour. Stir and cook the mixture about 8 minutes over medium heat. Add the lemongrass, coconut milk, ginger, pimento, thyme, and Scotch bonnet pepper to the pot. Sauté the mixture 2 minutes. Add the stock, bring the mixture to a boil, and then turn the heat down to maintain a steady simmer. Reduce the liquid by two-thirds.

Strain the soup, and return it to the pot. Add the cream, bring the soup to a boil, and serve immediately, garnished with crab meat.

Serves 8

Avocado and Ginger Vichyssoise

This soup was made famous by the Hotel Intercontinental in Ocho Rios.

1/2 cup unsalted butter or margarine
1 medium onion, finely chopped
1 ounce gingerroot, peeled and grated
1 large avocado, mashed
2 cups chicken stock
1/2 teaspoon salt
1 teaspoon ground black pepper
1/2 cup heavy cream
1 scallion, finely chopped

Melt the butter or margarine in a frying pan. Sauté the onions and grated ginger for about 2 minutes. Add the mashed avocado and chicken stock. Mix all the ingredients thoroughly, using a wire whisk to eliminate lumps. Simmer the soup for 10 to 15 minutes. Add the salt, pepper, and cream. Stir the soup, then remove it from the heat and let it cool. Chill the soup for at least 1 hour.

Before serving, chill six soup bowls. Garnish each bowl of soup with chopped scallions.

Serves 6

Susumber Soup

Susumbers are wild berries that are sometimes called gully beans because they are often found growing in the storm drains, or gullies, that divert the storm water through Kingston. Susumbers look like oversized capers and have a sour, bitter flavor.

1/2 pound dry salt cured beef
1/2 pound pig's tail
1/2 pound fresh beef
2 quarts water
8 dozen susumbers, cut in half
2 pounds carrots, diced
2 pounds turnips, diced
2 cho-cho squashes, peeled and diced
2 dasheens, diced
1 1/2 pounds yam, diced
1 thyme sprig
2 scallions
1 garlic clove
Salt and pepper to taste

Put the salt cured beef, pig's tail, and fresh beef into a large pot with 2 quarts of water. Bring the water to a boil, and simmer the meat for about an hour while you peel and dice the vegetables. Add the susumbers and vegetables, and continue simmering the soup. When the vegetables are almost tender, add the thyme, scallions, garlic, salt, and pepper. Simmer the soup for 1 hour longer, and serve.

Serves 8

Chapter 5

Jerks, Curries, and Rundowns

Jamaican Main Dishes

In the tropical heat of Jamaica, cooking often involves an outdoor fire. Whether it's smoldering pimento wood in a fire pit at the jerk shack or a tiny blaze underneath a ten-gallon can filled with curry goat or mannish water by the side of the house, Jamaicans like to cook outside.

Most of these recipes require some outdoor cooking gear. Jay likes a fifty-gallon oil drum cut in half and set on legs but you don't need to get that fancy. Anything that will hold a fire will work. Make yourself a rum punch and read this chapter out by the backyard grill.

Jamaican Jerk

Jamaican jerk, the barbecue with the strange name, has recently been discovered by the whole world. The way jerk pork, jerk chicken, and jerk seasonings are suddenly showing up in restaurants and supermarkets in the United States and elsewhere makes jerk seem like a new fad. In fact, jerked meat has been around for centuries.

Beef jerky, that staple of the American West, is jerked meat, too. The word jerk is believed to derive either from the Dutch *gherk*, which means pickled or preserved, or from the Spanish word *charqui*. The original purpose of jerk seasoning wasn't to make meat taste spicy, but to preserve it.

The early history of jerked meat in the New World is one of the most colorful tales in Caribbean history. The earliest purveyors of jerk were none other than the legendary buccaneers. They were named after the wooden frame they used to preserve their meat—the *boucan*, as the French called it.

In the early 1600s, escaped prisoners, runaway slaves, refugees, and other wild men hunted for wild pigs in the woods of Hispaniola. They made a living by curing pork and selling the meat to passing ships. So the tradition of jerked pork has been around for a long time.

Hunted by the Spanish, the buccaneers eventually gave up on the meat business, banded together, and went to sea. In the beginning, they did so for their own defense. But eventually they discovered that capturing Spanish vessels by surprise attack was a lot more lucrative than chasing wild pigs. The British hired them to defend Jamaica from the Spanish, and the rest, as they say, is history.

But Jamaica's own jerk tradition began with another group of people, runaway slaves who came to be known as the Maroons. They inhabited the desolate "cockpit" country of Jamaica, where they hid out from the British. Like the buccaneers, they hunted wild pigs and cured the meat on wooden frames. But the Maroons never made a business out of it; they left that to the present-day jerk masters of Boston Beach.

Today, jerk no longer means cured meat to Jamaicans. The term now describes the spice mixture that was once a preservative and is now a barbecue seasoning. But the tradition lives on in many ways.

True Jamaican jerk pork is still made using a whole, freshly slaughtered pig. The meat is coarsely chopped, then rubbed with the same kind of moist, spicy herbal marinade that has been used for centuries. It is then slowly roasted on a frame (metal has replaced green branches) over a pimento wood fire until the pork is well done with a crispy, crunchy crust.

But times are changing, and now that preserving meat is no longer the point, jerk seasoning is being applied to all sorts of foods. Today, any jerk stand in Jamaica will have both jerk pork and jerk chicken.

Recently, jerk fish and jerk lobster have become common on restaurant menus. The local snapper, jack, and parrotfish and the spiny Caribbean lobster are most often used. The jerk does not permeate the fish and lobster meat very deeply; it is used more as a seasoning than a marinade. The cooking time is also much shorter, so the jerk flavors do not meld as well as they do in traditional jerked pork.

Several good commercial jerk seasonings are available—Walker's Wood Jerk Seasoning, Real Jamaican Country Style Boston Jerk Seasoning, and Helen's Tropical Exotic's Island Fire Jerk Seasoning. These are quite acceptable, but not as good as freshly made jerk rub.

WELCOME TO BOSTON BEACH

Wet Jerk Rub

All the various wet jerk rubs, dry jerk rubs, and marinades have the same core ingredients: scallions, thyme, Jamaican pimento (allspice), ginger, Scotch bonnet peppers, black pepper, nutmeg, and cinnamon. Jamaican pimento (allspice) is essential; it is more pungent than allspice from elsewhere. The scallions used in Jamaica are more like baby red onions than the green onions we find in our produce sections. The thyme is a very small leafed, intensely flavored English thyme. These are the most critical herbal flavors in jerk seasoning; the next most important flavor is Scotch bonnet peppers.

Jamaicans all grow their own Scotch bonnets, or "country peppers" as they are sometimes called. Scotch bonnets come in several varieties, all of which have a similar "round taste," an intense heat with apricot or fruity overtones. The best substitute for a Scotch bonnet is a fresh habanero pepper.

1/2 cup fresh thyme leaves
2 bunches (about 15) green onions, finely chopped
1/4 cup ginger root, finely diced
3 Scotch bonnet peppers, stemmed and finely chopped
1/4 cup peanut oil
5 garlic cloves, chopped
3 freshly ground bay leaves
2 teaspoons freshly ground allspice
1 teaspoon freshly grated nutmeg
1 tablespoon freshly ground pepper
1 tablespoon freshly ground coriander
1 teaspoon freshly ground cinnamon
2 teaspoons salt
Juice of 1 lime

Combine all the ingredients into a thick, chunky paste. The mixture will keep in a tightly sealed container in the refrigerator for several months.

Most Jamaicans grind their spices by hand in a mortar and pestle. The whole spices tend to retain more aromatic oils in them and therefore more of a natural pungency. To save time, you can pulverize the spices in a spice grinder or coffee mill, and then add them to the other ingredients.

Yields 4 cups

Jerk pit at Boston Beach

The Jerk Process

Jerking is a two-step process. First you marinate the meat for at least four hours, preferably overnight. Then you slow-cook the marinated meat over hardwood coals.

Traditionally, a two-foot-deep pit is dug. Stones or cinder blocks are set at each end to support the green sticks for the grill framework. The fire is started, and, when the coals are ready, the green-stick grill is set in place. The jerk pork or chicken is placed on the grill about eight inches from the coals. Banana leaves used to be placed over the meat; nowadays, a sheet of galvanized zinc is usually used to help trap the smoky heat.

The meat is turned every 15 to 20 minutes to insure even cooking and prevent burning. Pork takes 2 to 4 hours, chicken 45 minutes to 2 hours, depending on the heat of the fire. The slower and longer the cooking, the better.

To make jerk at home, marinate the pork or chicken in the refrigerator overnight. Use a lot of jerk in proportion to the amount of meat—2 to 3 cups of jerk rub for a 6-pound pork roast. Instead of digging a pit, you can use a water smoker or a covered grill with a drip pan. It is best to have a drip pan directly underneath the meat to prevent scorching. If you pour half a bottle of Red Stripe beer into the drip pan, by the time the pork is done you'll have a great dipping sauce. Drink the other half of the Red Stripe while you're cooking.

For the fire, charcoal briquettes will work, but we highly recommend sweet hardwood for its flavor. In Texas we use pecan, apple, or peach wood; elsewhere, maple, walnut, almond, or hickory might be used. Start the fire with mesquite charcoal about an hour before you plan to begin cooking. When the coals are ashen, add sweet wood chips.

Jerked Pork

1 6-pound pork butt or loin roast
2 to 3 cups Wet Jerk Rub (see page 118)

Prepare the pork roast by placing it fat-side down on a cutting board and slicing it at 1 1/2-inch intervals to within one inch of the cutting board. Rub the jerk deeply into the roast. Marinate the pork in the refrigerator overnight.

Smoke the pork for 2 to 4 hours (depending on the heat of the fire) until the meat is crispy and well-done.

Serves 10-12

Jerked Chicken

1 1 1/2-pound chicken
1 cup Wet Jerk Rub (see page 118)

Cut the chicken in two. Pat the wet jerk rub onto both sides of the chicken halves. Marinate the chicken in the refrigerator for at least 4 hours. To set the jerk, sear the chicken halves on the hottest area of the grill until they are well browned. Move the chicken to a cooler area of the grill, and cook the meat 30 to 45 minutes, or until the juices run clear when the meat is punctured. The jerk rub should turn black and crusty.

Serves 2

Slash-and-Burn Red Snapper

Jerked fish is also called slash-and-burn fish. The name comes from the practice of "slashing" the skin of the fish to help the jerk flavors penetrate, and from the "burning," or charring, of the fish as it is slowly roasted.

1 whole red snapper (about 2 1/2 pounds)
1 cup Wet Jerk Rub (see page 118)

Clean, scale, and rinse the fish, and cut off the gill fins. With a sharp knife, make 1/4-inch deep vertical slashes about 1 1/2 inches apart along each side of the fish. Bend the fish so that the slashes on one side open to expose the meat, and pack each opening with jerk rub. Repeat on the other side. Marinate the fish in the refrigerator for 30 minutes.

Spread the rib cage open, and stand the fish directly on the grill or in a roasting pan. You can place a banana leaf or lettuce leaves under the fish to keep it from sticking. Smoke-roast the fish for 20 to 30 minutes until it flakes off the bone easily.

Serves 2

Jerked Turkey

Jay developed this recipe as an alternative to the usual U.S. holiday fare. Leftover Jerked Turkey makes awesome sandwiches and tacos.

1 11-pound raw unboned turkey breast
Basic Brine (see page 84)
1 1/2 cups Wet Jerk Rub (see page 118)

Soak the turkey breast in the brine overnight.

Remove the turkey from the brine, and rub it all over with the jerk rub, including under the skin. Smoke-roast the turkey over sweet wood for 4 to 6 hours. (This cooking time can be cut in half by removing the breasts from the bone, but the turkey will tend to be less moist.) When the turkey is firm to the touch, it is ready.

The turkey is best straight from the smoker with all the usual fixings.

Serves 12

Jerked Lobster

Spiny lobsters are cousins of the North American lobsters and crawfish. Slightly narrower than Maine lobsters, spiny lobsters do not have claws. The usual way to cook spiny lobster is to boil it for 10 to 12 minutes per pound in highly seasoned water. Spiny lobsters do not have as much fat as their cold-water cousins, so they tend to become dry and stringy if overcooked.

Jerked lobster is split, stuffed with jerk seasoning and butter, and then broiled instead of smoked.

1 spiny lobster
1 tablespoon Wet Jerk Rub (see page 118)
3 tablespoons softened unsalted butter

Split the shell of a spiny lobster down the middle of the underside. Stuff as much wet jerk rub as you can into the shell around the meat. Marinate the lobster for 1 hour in the refrigerator.

Just before broiling the lobster, stuff the softened butter into the shell. Broil the lobster until it is done, about 10 minutes.

Serves 1

Jerked Pork Sausage

While in Boston Beach, we got to try a little piece of freshly made jerk sausage. The vendor explained that he used only the choicest pieces of the jerk pork for the sausage and used the fresh intestine for the casing. More likely, he added yesterday's leftover jerked pork to fresh pork fatback. Nonetheless, the sausage was good, and it inspired Jay to create this recipe to use up leftover jerked pork, just in case such a thing should ever exist.

3/4 pound pork fatback
2 pounds lean jerked pork butt or
    pork loin
2 tablespoons chopped finely garlic
2 teaspoons fresh or dried thyme
1 teaspoon dry mustard
1 teaspoon coarsely ground or cracked
    pimento (allspice)
2 teaspoons coarsely ground or cracked
    black pepper
1 tablespoon kosher or coarsely ground
    sea salt
1/2 cup water
Medium hog casings

Coarsely grind the pork fatback (through a 1/4-inch plate of a meat grinder). Keep the fat cold. Finely dice the lean jerked pork butt, removing fat nodules and gristle. In a large bowl, mix the fat and meat with all the remaining ingredients except the casings. Knead the mixture with your hands until everything is well blended.

Stuff the sausage meat into the hog casings, and tie the casings into 4- to 6-inch links. This sausage will keep for 3 to 4 days refrigerated and up to 2 months frozen.

Yields 3 pounds

Note: If you have no sausage casings roll the meat into 1/2-pound logs in waxed paper. Refrigerate or freeze the logs, and cut them into sausage patties as needed. They are great for breakfast, with pasta, or as a stuffing.

Curry Powder

In the 1800s Jamaican curry was a kind of coconut rundown made by taking the jelly of a very young coconut, boiling it in its own water with a little cinnamon and adding curry powder to taste. Introduced by the British, it was not very common among poor Jamaicans.

That was before the East Indians came to Jamaica as indentured servants. Today, curries are very much a part of Jamaican cooking. Curry shrimp, curry lobster and the world-famous Jamaican curry goat are popular all over the island. Jamaican curry powder tends to be a tad hotter than Madras blends, with more hot mustard. Scotch bonnet peppers and Jamaican ginger powder add to the heat of Jamaican curries.

Making your own curry powder may seem a little extreme, but it is a wonderful lesson in the interplay of flavors and how the whole is greater than the sum of its parts. In Jamaica, all the ingredients listed here are available in the wild or at the market. By mixing and grinding spices in a mortar you will come to understand the amazing difference between freshly ground and store-bought curry.

If you can't find one or two of the ingredients, your curry powder will still be usable, provided turmeric is not one of the missing ingredients. A rhizome like ginger, but smaller and more yellow, turmeric is essential for a good curry powder.

5 parts ground turmeric
4 parts coriander seeds
3 parts cayenne
3 parts fenugreek seeds
2 parts cumin seeds
2 parts whole black pepper
2 parts star anise or aniseed
2 parts yellow mustard seeds
1 part whole cloves

1 part ground ginger
1 part grated nutmeg
1 part whole allspice

Combine all the ingredients. Store the curry powder in a tightly sealed jar away from light and heat.

Yields as much as you desire.

Fresh Green Curry Paste

Jay got this basic curry recipe from American chef Hugh Carpenter in a cooking class. Take the time to play with the mixture and adapt it to your personal tastes. Red curry paste can be made by using fresh or dried red chiles instead of the green serranos. Turmeric, cardamom, white pepper, and mustard seeds are other interesting additions.

8 whole cloves
24 whole black peppercorns
8 pimento (allspice) berries
1 teaspoon caraway seeds
1 teaspoon coriander seeds
1 teaspoon cumin seeds
10 minced garlic cloves
2 minced shallots
2 tablespoons minced ginger root
2 stalks lemongrass, minced
1 tablespoon minced galanga root
12 whole green serrano peppers, minced
1 cup fresh basil leaves, finely minced
1 teaspoon salt
1/2 cup vegetable oil

Put the cloves, peppercorns, pimento, caraway, coriander, and cumin into a 12-inch frying pan, and place the pan over medium heat. Cook, stirring, until the spices just begin to smoke and release their aromas, about 4 minutes. Then grind the spices into a fine powder using a coffee grinder or mortar and pestle. Combine the garlic, shallots, ginger, lemongrass, galanga, serranos, and basil. Add the salt and oil. Blend the ingredients in a food processor, or pound them in a mortar, until a paste is formed. Pack and tightly seal the paste in a glass jar with a film of vegetable oil over the paste.

Yields 2 cups

Jamaican Curry Goat

Mandeville curry goat is the standard by which all others are judged. Recipes vary, but one thing they all have in common is a freshly killed goat!

5 to 6 pounds goat meat, cut into
    1-inch cubes
6 scallions, very coarsely chopped
3 large onions, chopped
3 Scotch bonnet peppers, seeded
    and minced
1 teaspoon ground pimento (allspice)
About 1 1/2 tablespoons salt, to taste
2 tablespoons freshly ground
    black pepper
About 6 tablespoons Jamaican Curry
    Powder (see page 125), to taste
2 tablespoons unsalted butter
1/4 cup coconut or peanut oil
2 garlic cloves
4 cups water or chicken stock
1 cup coconut milk
Juice of 2 limes

Using your hands, mix the goat meat, scallions, half the onions, 1 to 3 peppers, allspice, salt, black pepper, and about 4 tablespoons Jamaican curry powder. Rub the goat well with the mixture. Now, as they say on the island, "You mus' put he down overnight"—which means let the meat marinate overnight in the refrigerator.

The next day, heat the butter in a large soup pot, and add the coconut or peanut oil. Add 2 tablespoons curry powder, and mix well. Add the garlic and the remaining onions, and brown them. Add the seasoned goat to the mixture. Mix well. Add the water or stock, the coconut milk, and the lime juice. Cover the pot, and let the meat simmer for 2 to 3 hours, until the meat is tender. Add a little more water if needed.

Serve the stew hot.

Serves 8

Note: Three Scotch bonnet peppers make this a really hot dish; you may wish to cut back to one or two peppers. Often carrots or new potatoes are added about 20 minutes before the curry goat is finished.

Curry Shrimp

In Jamaica, you are just as likely to get freshwater shrimp as you are the more familiar ocean shrimp. Valery Parchment ordered this curried shrimp dish at the Fish Place in Kingston. She's lucky she got any after we started "tasting" it.

1/4 cup unsalted butter
3 onions, finely diced
1 cho-cho squash, peeled and diced
2 garlic cloves, minced
2 tablespoons Jamaican Curry Powder
    (see page 125)
3 tablespoons flour
1 cup Red Stripe beer or shrimp stock
Juice of 1/2 lime
1 bay leaf
1 teaspoon whole black peppercorns
1/2 tablespoon peeled and minced
    ginger root
3 scallions, finely chopped
Salt and pepper to taste
2 pounds raw shrimp, peeled and
    deveined

In a large, heavy skillet, melt the butter. Add the onions, cho-cho, garlic, and curry powder. Sauté the mixture for about 5 minutes, then sprinkle the flour over. Add the beer, lime juice, bay leaf, peppercorns, ginger, and scallions. Bring the mixture to a rolling boil. Add salt and pepper. Reduce the heat, and simmer the mixture, stirring occasionally, for about 20 minutes, until it is reduced by half.

Add the shrimp, cover the pan, and cook until the shrimp turn pink, about 5 minutes.

Serve the shrimp over a bed of rice and peas with a cold Red Stripe.

Serves 4 to 6

Curry Rabbit

Although there are some rabbits on the island of Jamaica, they are not commonly eaten. Jay makes this dish at his restaurant, though, and he says if people don't make it in Jamaica they ought to.

4 tablespoons flour
1/2 tablespoon powdered mustard
2 rabbits, quartered (about 5 pounds)
1/4 cup unsalted butter
2 onions, finely diced
3 carrots, sliced
2 to 3 tablespoons Jamaican Curry
    Powder (see page 125)
1 Scotch bonnet pepper
6 bay leaves
Leaves from 4 thyme sprigs
4 cups rabbit or chicken stock or water
Salt and pepper to taste
1 pound new potatoes, quartered
Juice of 1 lemon

Mix 2 tablespoons flour with the dry mustard, and coat the rabbit pieces with the mixture.

Heat the butter in a large, heavy skillet over medium heat. Add the rabbit pieces, and brown them evenly. Remove the rabbit pieces, and set them aside.

In the same pan, sauté the onions and carrots for about 3 minutes. Dust them with the remaining 2 tablespoons flour and the curry powder. Sauté for a few minutes more, then add the Scotch bonnet pepper, bay leaves, and thyme leaves. Return the rabbit pieces to the skillet and cover them with the stock or water. Cover the pan, and simmer the rabbit over low heat.

After an hour, add salt and pepper to taste, and add the potatoes. Simmer for another hour.

When the meat is starting to fall off the bone, add the lemon juice, and serve.

Serves 8

The Lobster Boys

When I was about 15 my Uncle Richard let his son Andrew and me borrow his boat to go out to the islands off Kingston harbor. My cousin and I grabbed some pots, rice, cooking oil, seasonings, and fresh water, and headed out on our adventure.

We didn't take any other food with us; the plan was to live off the land. By the time we got out to the key, we were starving! We dropped anchor, and in getting off the boat we literally stepped into a lobster nest.

Twenty or thirty lobsters shot out from underneath the coral head we were standing on. We both started grabbing lobsters with our bare hands and throwing them up on the beach. In no time at all we had a fire going. We roasted lobsters in the shell over the open flames, then we found the pot and got the water boiling, and cooked more lobsters in rice. We ate like kings that weekend.

Uncle Richard, who expected us to come back hungry, was shocked that we had some lobsters left over to give him!

—Jay McCarthy

Curry Lobster

When we stopped for lunch at the White Horse Grill on the way to Black River, we had just ordered some beer when a man pulled up on a scooter with a potato sack. Without saying a word he handed the sack over to the cook, who took it around to the back of the house. Curiosity got the best of us, and we followed her.

In her open-air kitchen, next to the grill, the cook had set the now moving potato sack. Seeing our curious faces, she reached in and produced several glistening, snapping spiny lobsters. We immediately returned to our table and ordered the curry lobster. Then we went back to the kitchen to watch her prepare it.

1/4 cup vegetable oil
1 very ripe plantain, diced
1 large tomato, chopped
1 onion, chopped
2 scallions, finely chopped
1 garlic clove, minced
2 to 3 tablespoons Jamaican Curry
   Powder (see page 125)
1 cup water
2 pounds raw lobster meat, cut into
   1-inch pieces
Salt and pepper to taste
2 tablespoons unsalted butter

Heat the oil in a large, heavy skillet, and add the plantain, tomato, onion, scallions, garlic, and curry powder. Sauté for 5 minutes. Slowly pour in the water, and stir. When the liquid starts to simmer, add the lobster meat. Cover the skillet, reduce the heat, and simmer gently for 12 to 15 minutes.

Add salt and pepper to taste. Stir in the butter, remove the skillet from the heat, and serve.

Serves 4

Jamaican Curried Chicken

Depending on where in Jamaica you ask how to make curried chicken, you will probably be told one of two techniques. The first is to rub the chicken with limes, dust with curry powder, and let the chicken sit overnight before cooking. The second is to sear the chicken before adding any of the other ingredients. Whichever technique you choose to employ, the addition of a whole Scotch bonnet pepper during the simmering will guarantee a spicy chicken. Enjoy.

2 3-pound chickens, cut into 8 pieces
    each
Juice of 1 lime
1/4 cup coconut oil
3 garlic cloves, minced
3 scallions, chopped
1/2 teaspoon freshly ground black pepper
1 tablespoon Jamaican Curry Powder
    (see page 125)
1 teaspoon ground pimento (allspice)
3 thyme sprigs
1 ounce gingerroot, peeled and finely
    diced
1 cup coconut milk
1 cho-cho squash, peeled
2 carrots, sliced 1/8-inch thick
1 potato, peeled and 1-inch diced

Either (1) soak the chicken with the lime juice, sprinkle with curry powder, and marinate the chicken overnight, or (2) sear the chicken in a hot pan, then remove it. Pour the lime juice over it, and set it aside.

In a "dutchy" (dutch oven), heat the coconut oil. Add the garlic, scallions, black pepper, curry powder, pimento, thyme, and ginger, and cook till the scallion is bright green. Add the chicken (whether marinated or seared) and simmer it, covered, over low heat for about 10 minutes. Add the coconut milk, cho-cho, carrots, and potatoes. Cook the mixture for 30 to 40 minutes, covered.

Serve the curry over rice and peas (see page 164).

Serves 6

Braised Ginger Pork
with Red Hills Ortaniques

An ortanique is a cross between an orange and a tangerine.
If you can't find any ortaniques, you'll get the same effect by
mixing equal parts fresh orange juice and fresh tangerine juice.

2 pounds lean pork, cubed
Flour, for dredging the pork
3 tablespoons vegetable oil
1/3 cup soy sauce
1/3 cup ortanique juice
2/3 cup chicken stock
1/4 cup dry sherry
1/2 cup finely diced onion
1 garlic clove, minced
1/2 cup finely chopped scallion
2 tablespoons sugar
1/4 cup thinly sliced ginger root
Pinch ground white pepper

Dredge the pork in the flour, and shake off the excess. Heat the oil in a large, heavy skillet over medium heat. Brown the pork. Drain off the excess fat. Add the soy sauce, ortanique juice, stock, and sherry to the pan. When the mixture comes to a simmer, add the onion, garlic, scallion, sugar, ginger, and pepper. Simmer, covered, for 20 minutes, or until the meat is tender.

Serve the pork over rice and peas (see page 164).

Serves 4

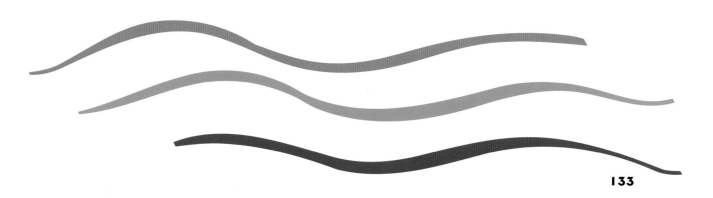

Hell on Top, Hell on the Bottom, Hallelujah in the Middle (Turned Cornmeal)

Cornmeal that is boiled and "turned" over the fire is a very old Jamaican country dish. It is seasoned in different ways all over the island. Jay's Aunt Hilda always made "turned corn" on Sundays because she had a big family with many friends. The dish made it easy to expand a meal for five to serve as many as twenty.

The crazy name—Hell on Top, Hell on the Bottom and Hallelujah in the Middle—comes from the method of cooking. The cornmeal is made in a "dutchy," a cast-iron dutch oven. The dutchy is placed over hot coals with more hot coals heaped on top of the cast-iron lid. "Hallelujah" describes what's inside the pot.

1/4 cup diced salt pork
1/4 cup vegetable oil for frying
1 onion, chopped
2 scallions, chopped
6 okra pods, sliced
2 medium tomatoes, diced
2 thyme sprigs
1/2 Scotch bonnet pepper, diced very fine
1/4 cup saltfish (salt cod), soaked in
    water for 20 minutes, and then diced
    or shredded fine
1/4 pound unsalted butter
4 cups coconut milk
Pinch of ground black pepper
2 cups cornmeal

Fry the salt pork until it is golden brown. Discard the melted fat, and set the salt pork pieces aside.

In the same pan, heat the oil. Sauté the onion, scallions, okra, tomatoes, thyme, and Scotch bonnet pepper until the vegetables are soft. Stir in the salt pork, saltfish, and butter.

Pour the coconut milk into a heavy pot or the top of a double boiler. Add the black pepper and the salt pork-saltfish-vegetable mixture. Bring the ingredients to a boil, and simmer until a slight scum appears on the surface, or about 10 minutes. Add the cornmeal, stir well, then cover the pot. If you are using a cast iron pot with a lid, it can be put on hot coals with more coals heaped on the lid for 20 to 30 minutes or steam the mixture for about a half hour over very low heat, stirring or "turning" occasionally.

Grease an ovenproof glass dish and "turn" the cornmeal firmly into it. Cover the dish, and keep it warm until you serve it.

Unmold the turned corn. Aunt Hilda often served it with stewed chicken.

Serves 8

Saltfish and Ackee

This traditional Jamaican breakfast originated in the days of the British, when the law decreed that every year each slave must be given an allotment of salt cod from New England.

Tourists are inevitably offered a breakfast of ackee and saltfish, which they often mistake for scrambled eggs at first and then avoid for the rest of the trip. Jamaicans, however, become vexed when they travel abroad and find that salt fish and ackee is unavailable. To each his own.

2 dozen ackees
1/2 pound saltfish (salt cod)
1/3 cup coconut oil
1/4 to 1/2 Scotch bonnet pepper, finely chopped
1/2 teaspoon ground black pepper
3 scallions, finely chopped
4 medium tomatoes, finely diced
3 medium onions, finely diced

Remove all the seeds and membranes from the ackees. Put them into a saucepan, cover them with lightly salted water, and boil them for about 20 minutes. Drain the ackees, and keep them warm.

Wash the saltfish, place it in a saucepan, and cover it with cold water. Boil until the fish is tender, about 15 to 20 minutes. Pour off the water, remove all the skin and bones from the fish, and flake the fish. Set the fish aside, and keep it warm.

In a large, heavy pan, heat the coconut oil. Add to it the scotch bonnet pepper, black pepper, scallions, tomatoes, and onions. Cook for about 4 to 5 minutes over medium heat. Add the saltfish, and stir gently. Add the reserved ackees, and toss gently.

Serve Saltfish and Ackee with Johnny cakes.

Serves 4 to 6

Escoveitch Fish

Escoveitch Fish, or "fried fish and bammy," are sold all over the island of Jamaica, but Old Harbor and Port Royal are the two places best known for their "fish ladies." The fish ladies are vendors who compete for business from their closely grouped stalls. Each lady has a glass box with two or three different types and sizes of fried fish—usually small parrot fish, grunt, and snapper. Snapper tends to be the most expensive. You pick the fish you want, and it is either wrapped in paper or put in a plastic bag. Then the "escoveitch," or pickled hot pepper juice, is drizzled over the fish. The bammy, whole or half, is purchased separately.

3 pounds small whole fish, or a large fish cut into 1/2-inch slices
2 limes, sliced
1 tablespoon salt
2 tablespoons freshly ground black pepper
1/4 cup flour
1 cup coconut oil or vegetable oil
2 bay leaves
1/2 cup malt vinegar
1 cho-cho squash, peeled and cut into thin strips
1 ounce gingerroot, sliced
1 teaspoon pimento (allspice) berries
2 large onions, sliced
2 Scotch bonnet peppers, sliced

Wash the fish thoroughly in cold water, pat it dry, and rub it with the lime slices. Then season it with the salt and pepper. Allow the fish to rest for 30 minutes.

Lightly dust the fish with flour. Heat the oil in a large skillet, and fry the fish on both sides until it is crisp and brown. Set the fish aside to cool.

In a saucepan, combine the bay leaves, vinegar, cho-cho, ginger, pimento, onions, and Scotch bonnet peppers, and cook until the onions are tender. Let the mixture cool, then pour it over the fish, and cover the pan. Marinate the fish for at least two hours at room temperature.

Serve the fish chilled or at room temperature. Spoon the marinade over each serving.

Serves 6

YS Grilled Pompano

The YS Papaya Plantation is the home of the absolutely amazing YS Falls. Stopping to see the falls, we arrived carrying a pompano we had bought that morning in the Black River Market. We asked our host, Simon Browne, if we could get our pompano cooked. He gave it to the grill man, who cut it into steaks, slathered it with fruit sauce, and cooked it over hot coals. Those pompano steaks were unforgettable.

5 pounds pompano steaks
2 limes, sliced
Salt to taste
1/2 pawpaw (papaya), peeled and puréed
1/2 cup Wet Jerk Rub (see page 118)
1/4 vegetable oil

Rub the pompano steaks on both sides with the limes, and sprinkle them with salt. Combine the papaya purée, jerk rub, and oil. Cover the steaks with the mixture, and let them marinate for 5 minutes.

Grill the fish slowly over medium heat till the meat starts to flake from the bone.

Serve the fish with rice and peas (see page 164).

Serves 6

Fish Story

One summer, when I was old enough to help the crew, I got to go along with my Uncle Richard to compete in the world-famous Port Antonio Marlin Fishing Tournament. The biggest marlin we caught that year was six and a half feet from tip to tail and about 160 pounds. It wasn't even a contender.

But the Port Antonio Yacht Club was a great place to eat dinner at that time of year. We all brought our marlin there and turned them over to the kitchen. That's where I ate my first marlin steak. It was an inch thick and weighed at least 18 ounces. The meat was pearly white, with iridescent colors shining in the moisture of the grain. Grilled a little rare, it had a luxurious, succulent texture. It has been almost twenty years since I tasted that first "steak," and thinking of it still makes me salivate.

—Jay McCarthy

Grilled Marlin

If you can find fresh marlin, go for the thickest steaks available. Grill the fish a little rare; it toughens quickly if overdone. Serve it with a little salsa and some rice and peas; with fish this good, the simpler the presentation, the better it tastes.

Salt and pepper to taste
2 pounds thick marlin steaks
Juice of 2 limes
1 garlic clove, minced
1/4 cup vegetable oil

Salt and pepper the marlin steaks. Combine the lime juice, oil, and garlic in a bowl and turn the steaks in this mixture. Let them marinate for 5 minutes.

Grill the steaks quickly over a fairly hot fire—about 10 minutes for a 1-inch steak, 5 minutes for a 1/2-inch steak.

Serve the steaks at once.

Serves 4

Mackerel Rundown

A rundown is a dish that's been reduced by slow cooking. The term comes from the Jamaican description of the process. "You cook it til it rundown." The ingredients almost always include coconut milk which provides the thickening.

3 pounds pickled mackerel
Flesh of 2 large coconuts, grated
9 cups water
1 teaspoon ground black pepper
2 whole green Scotch bonnet peppers
3 garlic cloves, minced
6 tomatoes, chopped
2 onions, chopped
5 scallions, chopped
3 thyme sprigs
9 green bananas, peeled, split lengthwise

Soak the mackerel in cold water overnight.

Discard the water, and remove the fins, side bones, and heads from the fish. Cut the fish into 1-inch-wide pieces.

In a large bowl, add the 9 cups water to the grated coconut, and stir. Strain the coconut milk through a fine sieve. Discard the solids (the "trash"). In a saucepan, bring the coconut milk to a boil. Add the black pepper, Scotch bonnet peppers, garlic, tomatoes, onions, scallions, and thyme. When a film begins to form on the coconut milk, add the pickled mackerel meat and the green bananas. Continue to cook until the bananas are done, about 15 to 20 minutes.

Rundown is served for breakfast or lunch with steamed callaloo or roasted yams.

Serves 6

Jamaican Stewed Chicken

Jamaicans use yard chickens or old layers when they make this recipe. To get the same sort of flavor use a "free-range" chicken or a stewing hen.

1 5- to 6-pound stewing chicken
1 to 2 large onions, chopped
1 ounce gingerroot, sliced fine
1 teaspoon ground black pepper
1 teaspoon salt
1/4 cup vegetable oil
3 tomatoes, diced
2 garlic cloves, minced
1 whole green Scotch bonnet pepper
1 teaspoon paprika
3 to 4 thyme sprigs
1 tablespoon Pickapeppa Sauce
2 tablespoons hot water

Rinse the chicken and pat it dry. Season with one onion, the black pepper, the salt, and the ginger. Refrigerate the chicken overnight.

The next day, cut the chicken into six or eight pieces.

In a large, heavy pan, heat the oil. Brown the chicken on all sides. Lower the heat, and add the remaining chopped onions, and the tomatoes, garlic, Scotch bonnet pepper, paprika, thyme, Pickapeppa, and hot water. Cover the pan, and simmer the chicken 20 to 30 minutes, adding a small amount of water as necessary. The chicken will be fork-tender when done.

Serves 6

Scotch bonnet pepper sauce

Chapter 6

Scotch Bonnets, Chutneys, and Banana Jam

Jamaican Sauces and Seasonings

Hot sauces, chutneys and fruit preserves are popular plate pepper-uppers at Jamaican tables. We've collected some of our favorites in this chapter.

The glazes, cures and oils suggested here are not authentic Jamaican recipes; they are Jay McCarthy's own concoctions. As a professional chef and a native son of Jamaica, Jay couldn't resist finding some new ways to use his favorite Jamaican ingredients. When you come home from Jamaica with a bunch of fresh pimento leaves in your suitcase, you have to come up with a recipe like Pimento Leaf Oil to put them to good use before they dry out. They don't need Pimento Leaf Oil in Jamaica, because they always have fresh pimento leaves, but we thought you might appreciate these ideas for using Jamaican ingredients.

One Jamaican ingredient that is turning up in grocery stores everywhere lately is the Scotch bonnet pepper. The scotch bonnet is at the center of the Jamaican seasoning universe. Jamaican table sauces always seem to include this fiery pepper in some shape or form. Whether it's in the ubiquitous shaker bottle with carrots, onions, ginger, and vinegar that you shower all over everything, or in a more subtle blend like Pickapeppa's combination with tomatoes and tamarinds, this pepper is going to get you one way or another.

We found five or six different cultivars of the pepper in Jamaica. Some are tiny and bullet-shaped; others are rounder and look more like habaneros. The classic Scotch bonnet has a wavy ridge around the middle, so it looks like a cap, which is why it got its name. Scotch bonnets range in color from green to orange to bright red.

In all their different shapes, Scotch bonnets are often called "country peppers" in Jamaica, because the country folk grow them in their gardens and around their houses. All of the cultivars are varieties of *Capsicum chinense*, a species of pepper that originated in South America. The habanero of Mexico and the datil pepper of Florida are other members of this pepper family. They all have one thing in common—they are the hottest peppers in the world.

Scotch bonnets are so potent that many recipes call for them to be simply dropped into the soup or stew while it cooks and removed and discarded afterwards. And even that much contact with the food is sometimes enough to make a soup or stew too hot.

Scotch Bonnet Pepper Sauce

Handle Scotch bonnets with extreme caution. It's best to wear gloves when cutting and cleaning them. The tiniest drop of pepper juice on your hands can result in incredible pain should you inadvertently wipe your face or rub your eye. Enjoy this Scotch bonnet sauce, but use it sparingly!

1 tablespoon vegetable oil
2 onions, diced
2 ripe mangoes or pawpaws (papayas), skinned, seeded, and diced to 1/2 inch
6 carrots, diced
2 cho-cho squashes, peeled and diced
12 pimento (allspice) berries
10 whole black peppercorns
4 thyme sprigs
1 ounce gingerroot, finely diced
1/2 cup sugar
8 to 12 Scotch bonnets
1/4 cup cane or cider vinegar

In a nonreactive pot, heat the oil. Sauté the onions until they are translucent but not brown. Add the mangoes or pawpaws, carrots, cho-cho, pimento berries, peppercorns, thyme, and ginger. Sauté the mixture 5 minutes, stirring constantly. Add the sugar and Scotch bonnet peppers. When the sugar has become syrupy, add the vinegar, and cook until the carrots are soft, about 5 to 10 more minutes.

Purée the mixture in a blender, and strain it. Store it in a tightly closed bottle in the refrigerator.

Yields 3 to 4 cups

Spirit's Pepper Sauce

Spirit Taylor is known as the Spiceman in Boston Beach, a Jamaican town famous for its jerk. Spirit, who supplies a lot of the spices that the locals use for their secret jerk recipes, grinds his dry ingredients in an ancient meat grinder worn from decades of use. This recipe is inspired by his respect for spices and spiciness.

2 finger-length pieces Jamaican
    cinnamon bark
10 pimento (allspice) berries
10 whole black peppercorns
1/4 nutmeg seed, with mace
4 cinnamon leaves
4 pimento (allspice) leaves
6 red Scotch bonnet peppers, finely
    diced
3 medium onions, finely diced
2 medium carrots, finely diced
4 garlic cloves, minced
1 teaspoon ketchup
1 teaspoon Pickapeppa Sauce
2 tablespoons dark rum
2 cups cane or cider vinegar

Grind all the dry ingredients in a mortar or a spice or coffee grinder. Put the red Scotch bonnets, onions, carrots, and garlic into a small nonreactive saucepan. Add the ketchup, Pickapeppa, dark rum, vinegar, and spices, and bring the mixture to a boil, stirring occasionally. Allow the sauce to cool, then put it into a bottle. It will keep for several months in the refrigerator.

Use the sauce sparingly to accompany stews, grilled meats, or whatever you feel could use a bit of Spirit.

Yields 2 cups

"Spirit" Taylor, Boston Beach

Pawpaw-Pepper-Mustard Sauce

This sauce is great on grilled chicken or as a dipping sauce for raw vegetables.

1 pawpaw (papaya), halved, peeled, seeded, and diced
1 tomato, diced
1/2 cup diced onion
2 Scotch bonnet peppers, stemmed, seeded, and chopped
1/2 cup red wine vinegar
1/4 cup white wine
2 tablespoons Dijon mustard

2 tablespoons brown sugar
2 tablespoons Worcestershire sauce
1 teaspoon red hot sauce, such as Tabasco

In a blender, purée all the ingredients together. Warm the sauce before serving.

Yields 2 cups

Gingered Banana Chutney

The word *chutney* comes from the East Indian *chatni*. These sweet and savory sauces, made with fruit, spices and vinegar, are the traditional accompaniment to curry. They are part of Jamaica's Indian heritage, although the English introduced the use of chutney on toast or crackers and as a complement to cheese. Chutneys are also excellent with grilled meats and fish.

Jamaica's bounty of tropical fruits and fresh spices makes the island's chutneys especially flavorful. Here is a uniquely Jamaican version of this classic Indian sauce.

1 tablespoon coconut oil or peanut oil
1 onion, thinly sliced
1 tablespoon fine julienne or diced
    gingerroot
4 slightly underripe bananas, split in half
    lengthwise and sliced 1/2 inch thick
Juice of 1 lemon
1/4 cup malt or cider vinegar
1/4 cup orange juice
1 teaspoon freshly cracked black pepper
Pinch of freshly grated nutmeg
Pinch of ground or freshly grated
    cinnamon
Pinch of ground allspice
Pinch of salt

In a large frying pan, heat the oil. Add the onions, and sauté, stirring, until they are translucent, about 5 minutes. Lower the heat, and add the ginger. Sauté 1 minute. Add all the remaining ingredients, bring the mixture to a simmer, and reduce the heat to low. Cook the mixture to a thick sauce, about 10 to 15 minutes. Ladle the chutney into sterile jars.

The chutney will keep for about a week in the refrigerator.

Yields 3 cups

Pineapple Chutney

You could use a food processor to chop the pineapple, ginger, pepper, and onion, but a Jamaican wouldn't; the machine would tend to "mash e up."

3 cups pineapple, finely diced (reserve as much juice as possible)
2 ounces gingerroot, minced
1 Scotch bonnet pepper, minced
1 medium onion, cut into thin crescents
1 cup cane or cider vinegar
3 stalks lemongrass, peeled and cut into 3-inch pieces
1 cup dark brown sugar

Put the pineapple, ginger, pepper, and onion into a nonreactive saucepan. Add the vinegar, lemongrass, and sugar, stir-ring well to evenly mix the ingredients. Place the saucepan over medium heat, and bring the mixture to a boil, stirring constantly to avoid sticking. Reduce the heat to low, and continue to cook, stirring occasion-ally, until the chutney thickens, about 25 minutes. Pour the chutney into sterilized glass jars. It will keep refrigerated for up to 1 month.

Yields 2 cups

Watermelon Salsa

2 cups watermelon cubes, seeded
1/4 cup red onion, thinly sliced into crescents
Juice of 1 lime
1 tablespoon honey
1 tablespoon fresh mint, finely chopped
1 teaspoon red pepper flakes
Salt and white pepper, to taste

Toss all ingredients together. Season to taste. Serve immediately. The watermelon is best when crisp.

Yields 2 1/4 cups

The Pine Lady

When I was going to school in Mandeville, I always looked forward to lunch break. We bought our lunch from traveling vendors, who would come to the school to hawk their wares. Roasted peanuts, buns, homemade candies, and pepper shrimp were all for sale. But my favorite vendor was the "pine lady."

The pine lady would arrive with a big basket on her head, full to the brim with the most flavorful, juicy, sweet, perfectly ripe pineapples you have ever seen. You would tell her how much money you had to spend, and she would pick out an appropriately sized "pine." With a sharp knife, she would cut the top into a cone shape. Then, holding the pineapple by the cone handle, she would peel it perfectly in a blink of the eye. The best and more expensive "pines" were referred to as the "sugar loaves." Once you have tasted a sugar loaf pine you are spoiled for life, because all other pineapples will always seem to be lacking.

—Jay McCarthy

Lemon-Pineapple Glaze

Pineapple season in Jamaica is from May till July, the period when "pines" are at their peak of flavor. If picked early, the pineapples don't ripen; they rot. Perfectly ripe, golden pineapples are always the best.

6 to 8 ounces gingerroot, cut into long, thin strips
6 to 8 stalks lemongrass, cut into 3-inch pieces
2 vanilla beans, split
2 pineapples, 1/4 inch diced
6 to 8 cups sugar

Into a nonreactive pan, put the ginger, lemongrass, and vanilla beans. Measure the volume of the diced pineapples, add the pineapples to the pan, and add sugar in equal volume. Over low heat, cook the mixture, stirring, until the pineapples appear translucent, about 25 to 35 minutes.

Strain the mixture, reserving the pineapples. Return the syrup to the stove over medium heat. Slowly, reduce the syrup to the consistency of thick honey. Return the pineapples to the syrup, and ladle the glaze into sterile jars.

Yields 6 cups

Note: For a spicy twist, add some ground Scotch bonnet peppers to the syrup. This version is great over baked chicken or roasted pork.

Tamarind Glaze

This glaze is fantastic on chicken or turkey.

12 ounces tamarinds or 1 package
    (6 ounces) tamarind paste
4 cups water
8 each pimento (allspice) or bay leaves
2 tablespoons coriander seeds
2 tablespoons whole black peppercorns
2 cinnamon sticks
4 ounces gingerroot, chopped
2 cups honey

In a large nonreactive pot, heat the first seven items. Bring the mixture to a boil, and skim it. Boil, stirring occasionally until the volume is reduced by three-quarters. Add the honey, remove the pot from the heat, and strain the glaze. Brush it on grilled or roasted poultry.

Yields 3 cups

Note: Adding overripe mangoes or bananas takes this glaze to another level.

Jamaican Dry Sugar Cure

This cure is marvelous with beef tenderloin, but it also works well with almost any other meat.

3 1/4 cups brown sugar
1 cup white sugar
1/4 cup chili powder
1 1/2 cups paprika
2 tablespoons dried thyme leaves
2 tablespoons celery seed
2 tablespoons ground ginger
1/4 cup granulated garlic
1/4 cup dried oregano leaves
1/4 cup dried basil leaves
1 tablespoon cayenne
1/4 cup kosher or coarse sea salt

Mix all the ingredients together. Generously rub whatever meat you wish to cure with the mixture. Let the meat rest overnight, or for as long as 3 days.

Sear the meat in a hot cast-iron skillet or on a griddle, and then roast it to the desired doneness.

Covered, the leftover cure will keep indefinitely.

Yields 1 quart cure, good for about 40 to 50 pounds of meat

Annatto Oil

Jay loves to sauté cho-chos in this oil because they turn a wonderful bright yellow-green. Annatto oil is also good for coloring rice: Sauté the rice in oil for a few minutes before steaming.

3 parts peanut oil
1 part annatto seeds

Pour the oil into a saucepan, and heat the oil till waves appear in it. Remove the pan from the heat, and add the annatto seeds. Let the oil rest till it is cool.

Strain the oil, discarding the seeds.

Keep the oil in a tightly closed dark glass container away from heat and light.

Use the oil to color sauces, fillings, pastries, or starches. The oil will hold its color even at a medium-high heat.

Yields as much as you desire

Cinnamon-Thyme Oil

The better the olive oil, the more intensely the flavors of the spices are retained. Jamaican cinnamon bark is a lot stronger than commercially available cinnamon sticks.

1 finger-length piece Jamaican cinnamon bark (or 2 cinnamon sticks)
3 bird peppers
2 cups extra-virgin olive oil
10 thyme sprigs

Put the cinnamon, peppers, and oil into a small saucepan, and heat them over a low flame for 10 minutes to meld the flavors. Allow the oil to cool.

Put the thyme sprigs into a decorative bottle (the oil will keep longer in dark glass), and pour in the oil, discarding the peppers but retaining the cinnamon. Cork the bottle, and place it in a dark, cool place for 3 days.

Use this spicy herbal oil for basting, salad dressings, and marinades.

Yields 2 cups

Pimento Leaf Oil

This oil gives a refreshing twist to salads and marinades.

4 cups fresh pimento (allspice) leaves
1/4 cup pimento (allspice) berries
8 whole black peppercorns
3 cups peanut oil

Put the pimento leaves, berries, and peppercorns into a pot or other metal container. In a saucepan, heat the oil to about 180 degrees (it should not smoke).

Pour the oil over the leaves, and let the oil rest for 24 hours.

Strain the oil, crushing the leaves as you do so to release more flavor. Store the oil in a tightly closed bottle. The oil will keep, refrigerated, for up to 3 months.

Yields 3 cups.

Curried Ackee Sauce

Here's an unusual sauce that's great for a vegetarian feast or for serving with chicken.

1/4 cup unsalted butter or vegetable oil
1/3 cup finely chopped onion
1/4 cup flour
4 teaspoons Jamaican Curry Powder
    (see page 125)
1 teaspoon sugar
1 teaspoon finely grated ginger
1 teaspoon salt
Pinch of ground black pepper
2 dozen ackees, boiled and well drained
2 cups coconut milk
Juice of 1 lime

Melt the butter in a saucepan. Add the onions, and sauté till the onions are translucent. Remove the pan from the heat, and add the flour, curry powder, sugar, ginger, salt, and pepper. Stir till the ingredients are blended, and then add the ackees. Return the pan to the heat, and add the coconut milk a little at a time. Bring the mixture to a boil over medium heat, stirring constantly. Simmer for 1 minute, stir in the lime juice, and then remove the pan from the heat.

In a blender, purée the mixture. Strain it, and keep it warm until you are ready to serve.

Serve the sauce with rice or as an accompaniment for grilled or jerked chicken.

Yields 2 cups

Hibiscus Cream

This sauce is beautiful to behold, and tastes fantastic as well. Jay likes to serve it with fish or lobster.

1/2 cup dried sorrel (hibiscus flowers)
2 shallots, finely diced
1 cup white wine
1 stalk lemongrass, cut into 3-inch
    lengths
2 cups heavy cream

In a saucepan, heat the sorrel, shallots, white wine, and lemongrass. Boil the mixture until the wine is reduced by three-quarters. Add the heavy cream, and simmer for 15 to 20 minutes, or until the sauce appears thickened. Strain the sauce through a very fine mesh strainer, and keep it warm till you are ready to serve.

Serve the sauce with shrimp, fish, or lobster.

Yields 1 1/2 cups.

Preserved Tamarinds

Jamaicans love fruit preserves, and with the wonderful fruits available on the island it's easy to understand why. Jay's grandmother used to make preserved tamarinds or tamarind candy once or twice a year whenever she found really nice big tamarind pods at the market.

2 cups tamarinds, peeled and threads removed
3 cups sugar
1 cup water
1/4 cup molasses
2 ounces gingerroot, sliced thinly across the grain

In a saucepan, boil 1 cup sugar with the water, molasses, and ginger until a thick syrup forms.

In a large glass jar, layer the tamarinds with the remaining 2 cups sugar and so on until the jar is almost full. Then add the new sugar boiled down to a syrup, pour it boiling on the layers. It will be ready to eat in 2 weeks.

This is wonderful warmed up and served on ice cream.

Yield: 3 cups

Rose Apple Preserves

Rose apples, which have the delightful flavor of roses, make wonderfully aromatic preserves. These preserves are a great condiment for roast chicken.

24 rose apples, peeled and halved, with seeds and pith inner skin removed
2 ounces gingerroot, thinly sliced
2 cinnamon sticks
2 cups sugar
1/4 cup water

In a nonreactive pot, stew the rose apples, ginger, sugar and cinnamon sticks in the water till the rose apples are tender, about 30 to 40 minutes. Ladle the preserves into sterile half-pint canning jars, and seal the jars.

Yields 3 half-pints

Note: Crab apples and peaches also work well in this recipe.

Preserved Ginger

Although ginger is available year-round, it's best in July and August, when it is young and tender. It can get tough at other times of the year.

1/2 pound tender pieces of gingerroot
About 4 cups water
6 cups sugar
1 egg white (optional)

Bring a saucepan of water to a boil. Add the ginger root, and simmer it about 5 minutes to soften it.

Remove the ginger from the hot water and put it into a bowl of cold water. Discard the hot water or save it for cooking rice or chicken. Take the boiled ginger out of the cold water one piece at a time, and, holding the ginger over the bowl to catch any drippings of ginger juice, scrape the outer skin off. Put the scraped ginger back into the bowl and discard the skin. Unless you like your ginger spicy hot like Jay does, while you work at scraping, you may want to discard the ginger water and add fresh cold water to the bowl at frequent intervals. Remove the ginger, and put it into a nonreactive pot.

In a saucepan, make a thin syrup by heating 2 cups sugar with 2 cups of the ginger water. Pour the hot syrup over the ginger. Let the ginger sit in the syrup for 24 hours.

Drain the ginger. Make a thicker syrup by heating 2 cups sugar in 1 cup of the ginger water. Pour the syrup over the ginger, and let the ginger sit in the syrup for another 24 hours.

On the last day, make a very thick syrup with 2 cups sugar to 1/4 cup of the ginger water. Let the syrup cool. Drain the ginger, divide it among small jars, and pour the thick syrup over.

Yields 2 to 3 cups

Notes: If you prefer, all the syrup can be clarified with the white of an egg: In a saucepan, whip the egg whites till frothy. Pour the cold syrup over them, and bring the mixture to a simmer. Skim as necessary.

Also, you can use the same syrup each time, if you heat it to thicken it; this makes a very, very hot ginger preserve. By making fresh syrup each time, you reduce the heat considerably. The second day's ginger syrup can be used in an interesting variation on Coffee Pecans (see page 207).

159

Otaheïte Apple Stew

As a boy, Jay knew every Otaheïte apple tree within four miles of his house intimately. He knew how many apples they had, how many were ripe, and how many he could eat. Invariably there was an abundance for a while and then none. This stew was one method of preserving Otaheïte apples for times when none were to be found.

24 very ripe Otaheïte apples
About 3 pounds sugar
1 ounce gingerroot
6 pimento (allspice) berries
1 cinnamon stick

Cut each fruit in half, and remove the stone. Weigh the fruit halves, then put them into a nonreactive pot with just enough water to cover them. Add half their weight in sugar. Stew the fruit until tender with the ginger, pimento, and cinnamon.

Pack the stew in sterile jars, and seal the jars.

Yields 4 cups

Note: This recipe works well with fish and a butter-cream emulsion.

Mammee Preserve

This preserve is great in a flan or served warm with cake and ice cream.

2 mammees
1/2 to 1 pound sugar

Peel the fruit, and remove the seeds. Slices the mammees, grate them, or slice one and grate the other. Weigh the prepared fruit, and put it in a saucepan with half its weight in sugar and enough water to cover. Boil the fruit.

Yields 2 cups

Tomato-Lime Preserve

This tastes great with grilled shrimp, or just spread on toast for breakfast.

8 to 9 large ripe tomatoes
About 3 1/2 cups sugar
2 limes, sliced
1/2 teaspoon salt
6 pimento (allspice) berries
3 whole cloves
Pinch of ground nutmeg
Pinch of ground cinnamon

Cut the stem out of each tomato. Cut a shallow cross in the bottom of the tomato with a serrated knife. Plunge the tomatoes into boiling water, and blanch them for 2 to 3 minutes, until the skins loosen. Remove the tomatoes from the water, and peel them. Cut the tomatoes into thick slices or wedges, and remove the seeds and juicy pulp. Weigh the tomatoes.

Put the tomatoes into a heavy nonreactive pot with half their weight in sugar and a little water. Add the limes, and simmer until the syrup thickens, about 20 minutes. Add the salt and spices, and simmer 10 to 15 minutes. Pour the preserve into sterile jars, and seal the jars.

Yields 6 to 8 cups

Banana Jam

Spread it cold on toast, warm it up and put on your pancakes, or try some on your chocolate ice cream. "Hey mon, now we be jammin'!"

1/4 cup light rum
2 cups water
1 cup sugar
1 1-inch slice ginger
6 bananas

In a saucepan, bring the rum, water, sugar, and ginger to a boil. While the syrup is boiling, peel the six bananas, and cut each banana in half. Put the halves into the syrup, and boil until the bananas are tender and the syrup is as thick as honey. Seal in jars.

Serves 6

Thyme salesman

Chapter 7

Garden Eggs and Jamaican Coat of Arms

Jamaican Vegetables and Side Dishes

The Rastafarians are Jamaica's most famous proponents of vegetarian cuisine, but in truth the whole island dotes on vegetable dishes. That's not very hard to understand, given the profusion of produce available all year round in the island's many markets.

The vegetarian tradition is also a carryover from the colonial days, when Jamaica's slaves were expected to grow their own food. They were given small plots of land, where they grew yams, callaloo, ackee, breadfruit, peppers, pumpkins, corn, and oranges.

The first vegetable markets were stocked with the slaves' surplus, which they were allowed to take into town to sell on Sundays. Although many of the vegetable dishes in this chapter are later innovations, most of them still rely on the same foods the slaves were growing in their garden plots at the end of the eighteenth century.

Jamaican Coat of Arms (Rice and Peas)

Jamaican Coat of Arms is the nickname for rice and gungo peas, perhaps the most common dish in all Jamaica. It goes with everything.

1 quart hot water
1 coconut, grated
1 cup gungo peas or kidney beans
1 garlic clove, chopped
2 scallions, finely chopped
3 thyme sprigs
Salt to taste
1/4 teaspoon ground black pepper
3 cups rice

Combine 2 cups hot water with the grated coconut. Squeeze out the coconut milk through a large strainer, add 2 cups more water to the coconut, and squeeze out the milk again.

Put the peas or kidney beans into a saucepan with the coconut milk, and add the garlic. Cook until the peas are tender but not mushy. Add the scallion, thyme, salt, black pepper, and rice, adding water, if necessary, so there is enough liquid to cook the rice properly. Cook the mixture, covered, over medium heat, stirring once or twice, until the rice is done.

Serves 6

Note: 2 to 3 ounces of salt pork can be added after the peas are cooked. Never add salt to peas until after they have cooked completely, or it will make the skins tough.

Callaloo

This Jamaican green is second only to rice and peas in the vegetable popularity contest. Used like spinach, callaloo turns up in all kinds of dishes, including the famous pepperpot soup.

6 bunches (2 to 3 pounds) callaloo, stemmed
1 tablespoon unsalted butter
1 onion, finely diced
2 scallions, finely diced
1 garlic clove, finely diced
Salt and pepper to taste

In a frying pan, melt the butter. Sauté the onion, scallions, and garlic, seasoned with salt and pepper, until the onions are translucent. Add the callaloo, cover the pan, and let it steam in its own juices. When the callaloo is bright green and wilted, it is ready to eat.

Serves 6

Note: Almonds added to this dish provide a surprising touch of flavor.

Ugli Callaloo

Ugli fruit is hybrid citrus fruit, a cross between a grapefruit and an orange. Juicy and pleasantly acidic, it complements the greens nicely. If you can't find an ugli, grapefruits are a good substitute.

12 to 16 ounces callaloo, stemmed and chopped
1 cup ugli juice
Salt and pepper to taste
1 tablespoon unsalted butter

Put the callaloo, with the salt, pepper, and ugli juice into a nonreactive pot. Add the butter, cover the pot, and steam the callaloo over medium heat for 10 minutes. Drain the callaloo, check the seasonings, and serve.

Serves 4

Roasted Garden Egg Purée

"Garden egg" is Jamaican for eggplant. Jamaican East Indians are very fond of "garden eggs," and grow a lot of them in backyard gardens. It is said that there is a difference between male and female garden eggs; the female ones are supposed to have fewer seeds and therefore taste less bitter. But no one has explained to us how to tell a male from a female garden egg without cutting it open.

Jay likes to serve this dish as a vegetable stuffing or dip. It is a great snack with fried plantain chips.

2 garden eggs (eggplants), peeled and sliced lengthwise 1/2 inch thick
1/2 cup Pimento Leaf Oil (see page 155) or olive oil
1/2 Scotch bonnet pepper, seeded and minced
6 garlic cloves, minced
Leaves of 6 thyme sprigs
1/4 cup vinegar
1 medium onion, sliced
2 tablespoons cracked black pepper
1 tablespoon soy sauce

In a bowl, mix the oil, Scotch bonnet pepper, garlic, thyme, and vinegar. Dip each garden egg slice in the marinade, and lay the slices on a baking sheet. Sprinkle them with the onion, pepper, and soy sauce. Pour the remaining marinade over the garden eggs. Let them marinate as long as overnight, or roast them immediately.

Preheat the oven to 375 degrees. Roast the garden egg slices for 25 to 35 minutes. (It is all right for the onions or garden eggs to brown.)

Grind the roasted garden egg slices, with their seasonings, in a blender, food processor, or meat grinder. Add more salt, pepper, or garlic to taste.

Serve the mixture with crackers or plantain chips, or use it as a vegetable stuffing for chicken or zucchini or winter squashes, or piped onto celery.

Yields 4 cups

Sister Fire's I-tal Rundown

Sister Fire runs a delightful open-air "garden of eating" above the beach at Fairy Hill. She serves her vegetable rundown as a main course with a beautifully flavored pumpkin rice (recipe follows). This rundown also makes a great side dish.

6 cups coconut milk (see page 164 {Rice and Peas})
1 pound pumpkin, peeled and cubed
6 carrots, finely sliced
1 pound potatoes, quartered
5 pimento (allspice) berries
3 garlic cloves, minced
3 scallions, chopped
2 thyme sprigs
2 to 3 cups water
5 annatto seeds
1/2 Scotch bonnet pepper
1/2 medium tomato, diced

Pour the coconut milk into a "dutchy" (dutch oven), and at a low simmer reduce it by half. Add the pumpkin, carrots, potatoes, pimento, garlic, scallions, and thyme. Add just enough water to simmer the vegetables without burning them. When the vegetables are almost tender, add the annatto, Scotch bonnet pepper, and the tomato and simmer about 10 minutes more before serving.

Delicious. Respect.

Serves 8

Pumpkin Rice by Sister Fire

4 cups coconut milk (see page 164 {Rice and Peas})
1 pound pumpkin (Big Mama squash), finely diced
2 sprigs thyme
2 garlic cloves
3 scallions, chopped
1 onion, chopped

1 whole green Scotch bonnet pepper
2 cups rice

Put everything except the rice into a "dutchy" (dutch oven). Bring the mixture to a boil, add the rice, and cover the pan. Simmer for about 20 minutes, and serve.

Serves 4

Stuffed Green Pawpaw

A lot of unripe fruits are treated as vegetables in Jamaican cooking. Green bananas, mangos, and pawpaws (papayas) are popular examples. This is one method of preparing a green papaya.

1 unripe (only slightly yellow) pawpaw
    (papaya), about 2 pounds
1/4 cup vegetable oil
2 onions, diced
2 garlic cloves, minced
2 medium tomatoes, diced
1 red bell pepper, diced
1 cup water and 1/4 cup water
2 ounces bacon or ham
1 Scotch bonnet pepper, seeded and
    diced
1 tablespoon bread crumbs
1 egg
Salt to taste

Cut off the top end of the pawpaw, and level the bottom end. Scoop out the seeds and discard them. In a frying pan, heat the oil. Briefly sauté the onions, garlic, tomatoes, and bell pepper. Add water until it is about 1/4-inch deep in the pan (about 1 cup), cover the pan and stew the mixture for 20 minutes.

Preheat the oven to 350 degrees. In a small frying pan, sauté the bacon or ham, and finely dice it. Mix it with the Scotch bonnet pepper, bread crumbs, egg, and salt. Add this mixture to the vegetable stew, then pack the stew into the pawpaw. Wrap the pawpaw in foil, set it in a small baking pan, and add about 1/4 cup water to the pan. Bake the pawpaw for an hour.

Unwrap the pawpaw, slice it into rings, and serve.

Serves 6

Note: The skin of the pawpaw should not be eaten; it contains an enzyme that can cause an allergic reaction.

Jay Corners the Breadfruit Market

While visiting Port Antonio after Hurricane Gilbert, I went for a walk with my family's gardener, Cecil. We saw a woman selling three "Port Antonio yellow hearts," the very finest breadfruit you can buy. I asked Cecil to purchase them for our dinner, as I was sure the woman would overcharge me. As I walked on while Cecil bartered, I heard a big commotion start up.

I turned to see poor Cecil being cussed up and down by another woman. Laughing, Cecil walked away with the breadfruit. When he caught up with me, he explained that the other lady was furious that he had bought all three breadfruit.

Gilbert had knocked down so many breadfruit trees that few of the fruit were available. When the woman had spied those three yellow hearts, she had gone all the way home to get her money—only to have Cecil buy all three just as she arrived back at the market. They were the first breadfruit I'd eaten in ten years, and probably the best I've ever had.

—Jay McCarthy

Roasted Breadfruit

Breadfruit was brought to the Caribbean by Captain Bligh. Records indicate that 347 breadfruit trees arrived on the HMS Providence on the fifth of February, 1793, and were distributed throughout the island. Breadfruit was intended to be used as food for the slaves.

1 breadfruit

Roast the breadfruit whole over charcoal (the best method), or directly over a gas burner. Turn the fruit as it begins to char. The roasting takes about an hour. When steam starts to escape from the stem end, the breadfruit is done.

Remove the breadfruit from the fire, and cut a circle at the stem end. Scoop out the heart, and discard it. Scoop out the meat, or cut off the charred outer skin, and cut the meat into slices, and serve it hot.

Stuffed Breadfruit

Dress up the rather bland taste of breadfruit with this tasty stuffing.

1 medium breadfruit, roasted (see above)
1/4 cup heavy cream
1 tablespoon unsalted butter
1 medium onion, minced
1 medium tomato, peeled, seeded, and
   chopped
Dash of freshly ground pimento (allspice)
Salt and pepper to taste

Preheat the oven to 300 degrees.

Scoop out the flesh of the breadfruit, leaving a shell at least 3/4 inch thick. In a bowl, mix the breadfruit flesh with the cream and butter, then add the onion, tomato, and seasonings. Stuff the mixture back into the shell, wrap the stuffed breadfruit with foil, and warm it thoroughly in the oven for 10 minutes.

Unwrap the breadfruit, and serve it whole on a platter. Guests should serve themselves.

Serves 6 to 8

Carving breadfruit in Boston Beach

Baked Cho-cho

The fruit of a climbing vine (*Sechium edule*) that grows all over the island, cho-cho is apparently kin to the melon family. It is eaten throughout Jamaica as a vegetable and is prepared in many different ways. In the United States, this pear-shaped squash is known as mirliton or chayote.

3 cho-cho squashes, peeled, halved
   lengthwise, and seeded
1 tablespoon unsalted butter
1 onion, finely diced
2 thyme sprigs
2 scallions, finely chopped
Salt and pepper to taste
1/2 cup bread crumbs
1/2 cup grated hard cheese like Parmesan
   or aged cheddar

Blanch (or, as they say in Jamaica, "quail") the cho-cho halves in boiling salted water for 8 to 10 minutes. Preheat the oven to 350 degrees.

While the cho-chos are cooking, melt the butter in a frying pan. Sauté the onions, thyme, and scallions, seasoning with salt and pepper. When the onions are translucent, remove the thyme sprigs, and add the bread crumbs. Remove the pan from the heat, and fold in the cheese.

Place the six cho-cho halves on a baking sheet, and divide the breadcrumb-cheese mixture among them, putting a little scoopful where the seeds were. Bake the cho-cho halves for 3 to 5 minutes, then broil them for 2 minutes, or until they are golden brown.

Serves 6

'Natta Cho-Cho

Jay loves to serve this vegetable side dish because of the vibrant color and unusual texture.

2 cho-cho squashes, peeled, seeded and
    cut finely julienne
1/4 cup Annatto Oil (See page 154)
Salt and pepper to taste

In a large skillet, heat the annatto oil over medium heat. Add the cho-cho, and sauté it for 3 to 5 minutes. Add the salt and pepper, and serve immediately.

Serves 4

Ackee-stuffed Cho-Cho

Stuffed cho-cho makes a great I-tal entrée or a filling vegetable side dish. The seeds of the cho-cho are edible; they make a nice garnish for salads, or they can be folded back into this stuffing.

3 cho-chos, peeled, halved, and seeded
    (reserve the seeds)
2 cups coarsely chopped cooked ackee
    (see page 214), or callaloo
3 scallions, finely chopped
1/2 cup grated cheese

Boil the cho-cho halves in salted water until they are tender but still firm, about 8 to 10 minutes. Preheat the oven to 375 degrees.

Place the cho-cho halves on a baking sheet. Distribute the ackee mixture over the cho-cho halves, and sprinkle with the cheese and scallions. Bake until the cheese melts and begins to brown.

Serves 6

Baked Plantains

A great change of pace from potatoes or yams, baked plantains make a wonderful starchy side dish for tropical meals.

4 plantains, well-ripened but not soft, peeled and sliced crosswise 1 1/4 inches thick
12 bacon slices
1/2 cup Lemon-Pineapple Glaze (see page 152)

Preheat the oven to 325 degrees. Wrap each piece of plantain with a half slice of bacon, and secure the bacon with a tooth-pick. Set the bacon-wrapped plantain cut-side up in a shallow baking dish, and bake until the bacon is crispy and the plantain is tender, about 25 to 35 minutes. A few minutes before removing the plantain from the oven, drizzle the Lemon-Pineapple Glaze over it.
Serve the plantain hot.

Serves 6

Fried Plantains with Chile

Jay got some plantains for his restaurant in Texas once, but they were extremely green. He let them ripen for about three weeks before using them. The last week his curious cooks reminded him daily about the by then black plantains, wondering when they could toss them in the trash. But the plantains were still firm. One day, they finally gave slightly to the touch. That was the day Jay fried them.

Here's a Jamaican plantain recipe with a touch of Texas in it. The ancho chilies may not be authentic, but they sure taste good.

6 plantains, well ripened but not soft, peeled and sliced lengthwise about 1/8 inch thick
2 dried ancho chiles (or 2 teaspoons chili powder)
1 tablespoon salt
1 tablespoon sugar
2 to 3 tablespoons vegetable oil
Salt and pepper to taste
1/4 cup flour

In a mortar or spice or coffee grinder, grind the chiles with the salt and sugar (or combine the chili powder with the salt and sugar).

In a heavy pan, heat the oil. Sprinkle the plantain slices with salt and pepper, then dust them with the flour, and fry them in the hot oil. When the plantains are brown on the bottom, turn them over. When they are almost done, sprinkle them with the chile, salt, and sugar blend.

Remove the plantains from the pan, and serve them warm.

Serves 4

Fufu

Fufu, a dish of green banana or plantain dumplings, was once very common in Jamaica. Fufu's origins can be traced to West Africa, where cassava and yam are still pounded into small balls called fufu. (The Jamaican Chinese have a sausage dish that is also called fufu.) This simple recipe can be jazzed up by adding diced jerk pork, a jigger of rum, or both.

4 green bananas or plantains
3 tablespoons soft unsalted butter
Salt and pepper to taste
1/2 cup finely diced jerked pork (optional)
1 ounce dark rum (optional)

In a large pot of water, boil the bananas or plantains in their skins for about 30 minutes, or until they are tender. Preheat the oven to 350 degrees.

Drain and peel the fruit. Pound the bananas or plantains in a mortar, or grind them in a food processor, to a smooth pulp, blending in the rum, if you like. Blend in the butter, salt, and pepper. Mold the pulp into small balls, adding the diced jerk, if you prefer. Place the balls on a baking sheet, and heat them in the oven for about 3 to 5 minutes. (Fufu can also be reheated by dropping the balls into boiling water.)

Serve the fufu hot.

Serves 6

Plantain Cakes

This is a sweet little side dish that kids go crazy over. Try them for breakfast sometime.

3 yellow firm plantains
1 tablespoon sugar
1 tablespoon finely grated coconut
1/2 tablespoon light rum
1/2 teaspoon baking powder
Vegetable oil, for deep frying

In a large pot of salted water, boil the plantains in their skins for about 30 minutes, or until they are tender. Peel them, and pound or purée them. Blend in the sugar, coconut, rum, and baking powder. Shape the mixture into 2-inch flat cakes.

Heat the oil in a heavy pot until it just starts to smoke. (The oil should be about 1/2 inch deep.) Fry the cakes till golden brown on both sides.

Yields 12 cakes

Jamaican Limbo Plantain

Everybody has heard the expression "Limbo lower now!" Well, that's the idea behind these flattened plantain chips.

3 tablespoons salt
4 cups cold water
2 large green plantains, peeled, and
    sliced into 1/2- to 3/4-inch rounds
3 cups vegetable oil

Dissolve the salt in the cold water. Add the plantain slices, and soak them for about an hour.

Heat the oil in a skillet over low heat. Fry the slices for a few minutes on each side, taking care that they do not brown. Remove them from the skillet, and, between pieces of waxed paper or a butter wrapper, roll each slice of plantain with a rolling pin, until completely flattened. (Just like the limbo, mon.) Return the flattened pieces to the skillet with the oil a little hotter this time, and fry the slices until they are brown and crisp.

Sprinkle the plantain chips with salt, and serve.

Yields 24 to 30 chips

177

Yam Balls

Jamaica has quite a few varieties of yams—the yellow or affoo yam, the negro yam, the white yam, the guinea yam, the hard yam, the Indian yam, the arracacha yam, and the Lucea yam. The white yam, sometimes called the "flour yam" for its starchy taste, is excellent roasted or boiled, then mashed with butter; the skin is fantastic roasted. The yellow yams, which vary from waxy to floury to stringy, are boiled or roasted, but their skins are rather bitter. The negro yam is large with a black skin and a white-yellow meaty texture. The Indian yam, or yampee, is somewhat sweet. The uncommon arracacha yam has a peculiar flavor, rather like parsnips. Introduced to Jamaica in 1822, it grows mostly in the Blue Mountains.

Under no circumstances is a sweet potato referred to as a yam in Jamaica. There are plenty of different yams in Jamaica without "confusioning" them with sweet potatoes.

1/2 pound negro yam
2 tablespoons softened unsalted butter
1 teaspoon ground black pepper
1 teaspoon salt
2 eggs, beaten
2 cups vegetable oil, for frying

Boil the yam in salted water for 15 to 20 minutes. Remove the yam, and mash it well with the butter. Add the black pepper, salt and eggs. Form the mixture into balls.

Heat the oil in a heavy pot. Fry the yam balls until they are golden.

Serves 4

Yam Pie

No, it's not a dessert like sweet potato pie; this is a Jamaican one-dish meal that may remind you of a tropical casserole.

1 pound ground beef or pork
2 tomatoes, finely diced
4 scallions, finely chopped
1 onion, finely diced
2 garlic cloves, minced
4 thyme sprigs
1 whole Scotch bonnet pepper
1 1-pound yellow yam, peeled
1/4 pound softened unsalted butter
1 egg, beaten
Salt and pepper to taste

In a heavy ovenproof pan, brown the ground beef. Drain off the excess grease. Add the tomatoes, scallions, onion, garlic, thyme, and Scotch bonnet pepper. Simmer the mixture 10 minutes.

In a pot, boil the yam in salted water until it is tender, about 20 to 25 minutes. Preheat the oven to 350 degrees.

In a bowl, mash the boiled yam with the butter, salt, pepper, and egg. Spread the mashed yam over the cooked ground beef. Place the pan in the oven, and bake the pie for 30 to 35 minutes.

Serve the pie hot.

Serves 4

Roasted Yellow Yam and Saltfish

Along the road from Kingston to Mandeville are many different road-side stands, selling everything from fried fish and bammies in Old Harbor to cashews and fresh orange juice in Clarendon. When you start up Melrose Hill to Williamsfield, you'll find an abundance of roasted yam-and-saltfish stands tucked away in the hairpin turns of the roadway. These stands have roasted yams all year round. Robb did not care for the dry-roasted saltfish and dry-roasted yellow yam served on a piece of dry paper bag, but Jay relished the childhood memories of past journeys along this road that the yam and saltfish brought back. He had no problem finishing Robb's portion.

1 2- to 4-pound whole yellow yam
1/2 pound saltfish (salt cod), soaked in
    cold water

Roast the whole yam slowly over coals. Drain the saltfish and warm it over the fire. When the yam is suitably charred all over peel it and serve it in 2-inch pieces along with pieces of saltfish.

    Serve the yam and saltfish on scraps of paper bag in cool mountain air.

Serves Jay or 4 other people

Jackass Corn

Jackass corn is a very hard, thin, crisp biscuit. Like the jackass, it is faithful, long-lasting, and tough. When you eat it, you sound like a donkey eating corn.

3 cups flour
1 teaspoon baking powder
1/2 teaspoon baking soda
1/4 teaspoon ground cinnamon
Pinch of ground nutmeg
Pinch of ground pimento (allspice)
Flesh of 1 coconut, grated
1 1/2 cups brown sugar
2 tablespoons unsalted butter, melted
3/4 to 1 cup water

Preheat the oven to 375 degrees.

Sift the flour, baking powder, baking soda, and spices together. Stir in the coconut and sugar. Make a well in the center, and add the butter and enough water to make a dough that can be rolled out on a floured surface.

Roll the dough to about 1/4 inch thick, and cut out 2-inch rounds. Place the rounds on an ungreased baking sheet, and bake about 25 minutes, until the biscuits are golden brown and crisp.

Yields 16 biscuits

Mrs. P's Cornbread

Jay's grandmother, Mrs. Parchment, makes an absolutely heavenly cornbread. Jay asked repeatedly for the recipe, but she always said, "Chile, I never wrote it down. I just make it, you know!" One day Jay caught her in the act and took some quick notes.

2 cups cornmeal
2 teaspoons baking powder
1/2 teaspoon baking soda
2 teaspoons salt
4 eggs, beaten
1 1/2 cups buttermilk
1 cup coconut milk
1 tablespoon vegetable shortening
1 red bell pepper, 1/4 inch diced
3 scallions, finely chopped
1/4 cup fresh grated coconut

Preheat the oven to 400 degrees. Sift together the dry ingredients. In another bowl, combine the eggs, buttermilk, and coconut milk. Slowly add this mixture to the cornmeal mixture; stir just until the dry ingredients are thoroughly moistened.

Melt the shortening in a 9-inch cast-iron skillet or "dutchy" (dutch oven) in the oven for 3 minutes, or until the shortening is very hot. Add the red bell pepper, scallions and coconut, and immediately pour in the batter. Raise the oven temperature to 425 degrees. Bake the cornbread for 35 minutes, or until it is lightly browned.

Serves 6

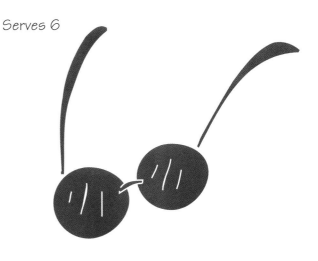

The Cartman's Hymnbook (Bulla)

It wasn't very long ago when donkey carts were the most common form of commercial transportation in Jamaica. Donkey carts loaded with bananas on their way to the shipping docks, or sugar cane on the way to the rum distilleries, clogged the roads of Jamaica fifty years ago.

And everywhere the cartmen went, they took their cartman's hymnbooks with them. Cartman's hymnbook, or bulla, is a brown cake made from the cheapest grade of flour and molasses, or "wet sugar" as it's known in Jamaica.

The oblong loaves looked like old-fashioned church hymnbooks. The busy cartmen didn't have time to stop for meals, so they always seemed to be eating this cheap, filling, and portable food while they drove their carts, hence the name.

3 cups flour
1 teaspoon baking powder
1/2 teaspoon baking soda
1/4 teaspoon salt
1 teaspoon ground cinnamon
1/4 teaspoon freshly grated nutmeg
1/2 teaspoon ground ginger
1/2 teaspoon ground pimento (allspice)
1/2 cup molasses
2 tablespoons unsalted butter, melted

Preheat the oven to 400 degrees. Sift all the dry ingredients together. Make a well in the center, and pour in the molasses. Add the melted butter, and lightly blend the dough. Turn the dough out onto a well-floured board, and pat it with your hands to a thickness of 1/4 inch. Cut the dough into circles, using a drinking glass or biscuit cutter. Lift the bullas with a well-floured spatula, and place them on a lightly greased, well-floured baking sheet. Bake the bullas for about 20 minutes or until the edges on the baking sheet are dark brown.

Serves 6

Note: Jay's grandmother baked her bullas on the waxed paper she saved from margarine or butter.

Boris Reid, owner of The Native
Restaurant in Montego Bay

Chapter 8

Matrimony, Gizzadas, and Mango Cheese

Jamaican Sweets and Desserts

Sweet things are everywhere in Jamaica. Fruits like custard apples and sweetsops are desserts that require no cooking at all. You simply open them up and eat the sweet pudding-like fruit inside. Watermelon, passion fruit, and papaya are ripe and ready when you are, too. But, if you don't mind doing a little cooking, a lot of prepared Jamaican desserts are well worth the effort.

Coconut is the star of a lot of these recipes; Jamaicans adore sweetened coconut confections like gizzada and coconut cream pie. Molasses and rum, products of the local sugarcane industry, also find their way into many Jamaican desserts.

The sharp tang of Jamaican ginger is another favorite flavor for sweets. Jamaicans like their ginger treats very spicy, the same way they like their ginger beer. Try the recipe for gingersnaps and you'll see what we mean.

And, of course, bananas are always a favorite in a country that has so many different kinds to choose from. But don't limit yourself to the usual—try some of these banana dessert recipes with red bananas or apple-like manzanos.

For an elegant dessert, Jamaicans head for the mountains—the Blue Mountains, where the world's finest coffee beans are grown. Coffee ice cream, coffee chiffon, or even a shot of Blue Mountain coffee liqueur poured over coconut ice cream is a great way to end a meal.

Here are a few sweet things from Jamaica we think you'll enjoy.

Matrimony

In the spring, when star apples and oranges are both in season, this smooth and silky dessert is a favorite on Jamaican tables.

4 star apples, seeded and sliced
   crosswise
2 oranges, peeled and sectioned
1/4 teaspoon freshly grated nutmeg
6 tablespoons sweetened condensed
   milk

In a bowl, mix the star apples, orange sections, and nutmeg. Stir in the condensed milk, and chill the mixture for a half hour before serving.

Serves 4

"Badda" Banana-Nut Bread

There ain't nuttin' "badda" than this sweet, moist banana bread. Loaded with raisins and nuts, it's great with Blue Mountain coffee.

1/4 pound unsalted butter, softened
1 cup sugar
2 eggs, well beaten
3 very ripe bananas, mashed (1 1/2 cups)
2 cups flour, sifted
2 teaspoons baking powder
1 teaspoon baking soda
1 teaspoon ground cinnamon
1/4 teaspoon ground nutmeg
Pinch of salt
1/2 cup milk
2 teaspoons vanilla extract
1/4 cup very coarsely chopped almonds
    or pecans
1/4 cup raisins

Preheat the oven to 350 degrees. Grease a loaf pan, and dust it with flour.

In a bowl, cream the butter and sugar. Blend in the eggs, then the mashed bananas. In another bowl, combine the flour with the baking soda, baking powder, cinnamon, nutmeg, and salt. Stir the flour mixture into the banana mixture, then stir in the milk and vanilla. Add the nuts and raisins last.

Put the batter into the loaf pan, and bake the bread for about an hour.

Yields 1 loaf

Sandra Forrester's Banana Bread

Here's a sweet style of banana bread that's served with dinner at the Bonnie View Hotel in Port Antonio.

8 (about 4 pounds) very ripe bananas
4 cups sugar
4 cups flour
16 eggs
1 1/2 quarts milk
Pinch of freshly grated nutmeg
Pinch of freshly ground allspice
Pinch of ground cinnamon
1 1/2 cups vegetable oil
2 teaspoons baking soda
1/2 teaspoon salt

Preheat the oven to 400 degrees. Lightly grease and flour two loaf pans.

Beat the bananas with the sugar, then beat in the flour until the bananas are dissolved. Add the 16 eggs in three stages, beating well after each addition. Add the milk and pinches of spices and beat again. Slowly beat in the oil, then the baking soda and salt.

Put the batter into the loaf pans, and bake the loaves until very firm, about 35 to 45 minutes.

Yields 2 loaves

Buying a gros michel banana at the Black River market

Gingerbread

The hot and spicy flavor of Jamaican ginger gives this more zing than most gingerbreads have.

2 eggs
3/4 cup unsalted butter, melted
1 cup Jamaican or other dark molasses
1 cup brown sugar
2 1/2 cups flour
1 teaspoon baking soda
1 teaspoon ground cinnamon
3 teaspoons ground Jamaican ginger
   (or 2 ounces fresh, grated)
1/4 teaspoon ground cloves
Pinch of grated nutmeg
Pinch of ground pimento (allspice)
1 cup boiling water

Preheat the oven to 350 degrees. Butter and flour a 9-inch cake pan.

In a large bowl, beat the eggs till smooth. Beat in the melted butter, and then the molasses and sugar. In another bowl, combine the flour, baking soda, cinnamon, ginger, cloves, nutmeg, and allspice.

Stir this mixture into the egg-sugar mixture. Lastly, stir in the boiling water.

Pour the batter into the cake pan. Bake the cake for 45 minutes to 1 hour, or until a knife inserted in the gingerbread comes out clean.

Yields 1 cake

Jamaican Bread Pudding

This is Jay's grandmother's recipe; her bread pudding was Jay's favorite dessert in his boyhood. You can substitute any white bread you like if you don't have Jamaican hardo bread.

1/2 loaf day-old hardo bread
1/2 cup sugar
1 teaspoon freshly ground cinnamon
1/4 teaspoon freshly grated nutmeg
1/2 cup dark rum
1/2 cup raisins
1/4 cup unsalted butter, melted
1/2 cup sweetened condensed milk
4 cups milk
6 eggs, beaten
2 tablespoons unsalted butter

Preheat the oven to 375 degrees. Butter a 9-inch ovenproof glass pie dish, or put the waxed paper from a pound of butter in the bottom of the dish. Tear apart the hardo bread into 1-inch-square pieces. In a bowl, mix together the sugar, cinnamon, nutmeg, rum, raisins and melted butter. Add the bread pieces, stir gently, and let the bread soak for a few minutes.

In another bowl combine the condensed milk, whole milk, and eggs. Add the bread mixture. Pour the milk-egg-bread mixture into the pie dish. Dot with the 2 tablespoons butter, and bake the pudding for an hour, or until a knife inserted in the middle comes out clean.

Serve the pudding warm or cold.

Serves 6 to 8

Hardo Bread

Hardo bread is a very dense white bread that's popular all over the island. The joke in Kingston is that the city's main flour mill is right next to the cement factory. People say that, when the wind blows the wrong way, the bread gets even harder.

Pink Drawers

This is a dessert version of dokono. The cherries make it pink.

2 1/2 cups sugar
4 cups coconut milk
5 cups rice
16 6-by-6-inch pieces of banana leaf
1 nutmeg, freshly grated
2 teaspoons vanilla extract
1 pound fresh Barbados cherries, pitted

Stir the sugar into the coconut milk. Stir in the rice. Let the rice soak in the coconut milk for a half hour. Dip the banana leaf pieces into boiling water, or heat them over an open flame, to make them pliable.

Add the nutmeg, vanilla and cherries to the rice and coconut milk. Divide the mixture among the banana leaf pieces, fold each piece of leaf into a packet, and tie each packet with a long piece of banana leaf or string. Drop the packets into a pot of boiling water, and simmer them over low heat for one hour.

Remove the packets from the water, and serve them hot or cold with Rum Syrup (see page 198).

Yields 16 dokono

Gingersnaps

Jamaicans love gingersnaps—particularly the "hot" ones— the ones that grab the back of your throat and say, "Welcome to Jamaica, mon, and have a nice day."

1/2 cup vegetable shortening
1/4 cup unsalted butter, chilled
About 1 1/2 cups sugar
1 egg
1/4 cup Jamaican or other dark molasses
2 cups flour
1 1/2 teaspoons baking soda
2 teaspoons ground cinnamon
2 teaspoons ground ginger
1 teaspoon ground cloves
1/4 teaspoon ground nutmeg
2 ounces fresh ginger, very finely diced
    (optional)

Beat the butter and shortening together. Gradually add 1 cup sugar, beating until the mixture is light and fluffy. Add the egg and the molasses, and continue beating until the ingredients are well mixed.

Sift together the flour, baking soda, and spices. Add the dry ingredients to the butter-sugar-egg mixture, and blend well. Add the fresh ginger, if you like, and mix it in well. Chill the dough for 2 hours.

Preheat the oven to 375 degrees. Shape the dough into 72 1-inch balls. Roll the balls in the remaining sugar. Place them on greased baking sheets, and lightly flatten the balls. Bake the cookies for 8 to 10 minutes, or until they are browned and cracked on the top. Place them on wire racks to cool.

Store the cookies in an airtight container.

Yields 72 cookies

Note: For an extra ginger bite, add some ground ginger to the sugar that you roll the cookie dough in.

Robb, in the lap of luxury on Jamaica's North Coast resort strip.

Easter Bun

This traditional Easter treat traces its history to the days of British rule.

1 yeast cake
3 cups milk, scalded
1 cup boiling water
1/2 pound unsalted butter, softened
1 cup brown sugar
1 teaspoon salt
1 whole nutmeg, grated
1 teaspoon ground cinnamon
1/8 teaspoon ground pimento (allspice)
1 egg, beaten
4 cups flour, sifted
1/4 pound crystallized cherries, chopped
1/4 pound raisins, chopped
1/4 pound crystallized citron peel, chopped
1/4 pound crystallized pineapple, chopped

Dissolve the yeast in a small amount of lukewarm water. Combine the milk and boiling water. Put the butter, sugar, salt, nutmeg, cinnamon, and pimento into a large bowl, and pour the milk-water mixture over. Beat in the egg. Add half of the sifted flour to the liquid, stir well, then add the yeast and all the fruit. Add enough of the remaining flour to make a stiff dough. Knead the dough about 3 to 5 minutes. Cover the dough, and let it rise until it has doubled in bulk.

Punch down the dough, sprinkle in the rest of the flour and knead well again. Shape the dough into loaves, place them in greased loaf pans, and let the dough rise again until it has doubled in bulk.

Preheat the oven to 350 degrees. Bake the buns until they leave the sides of the pans and are springy to the touch.

Yields 2 "buns"

Toto Cakes

The coconut turns this old variation on bulla into sweet coconut cake.

2 cups flour, sifted
2 teaspoons baking powder
1 teaspoon ground cinnamon
1/4 teaspoon ground nutmeg
1 cup sugar
1/4 pound unsalted butter
2 teaspoons vanilla extract
1 egg, beaten
2 cups fresh grated coconut

Preheat the oven to 375 degrees. Grease a shallow 9-by-13-inch baking pan.

Sift the flour, baking powder, cinnamon, and nutmeg together. In another bowl, beat the sugar and butter together until the mixture is creamy, and then beat it into the flour mixture. Add the vanilla, egg, and coconut, and mix the ingredients to a stiff, cookie-like dough. Spread the dough evenly in the baking pan, and bake for 30 to 35 minutes or until golden brown. Let the cake cool, then cut it into 24 squares.

Yields 24 pieces

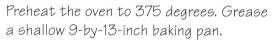

Fresh Coconut Cream Pie

If you like coconut cream pie, wait until you try it with fresh coconut!

1 cup sugar
1/2 cup cornstarch
1/2 teaspoon salt
3 cups hot milk
3 egg yolks, beaten
2 cups fresh grated coconut
1/2 teaspoon almond extract
1 teaspoon vanilla extract
1 9-inch baked pie shell
1 cup heavy cream

Combine the sugar, cornstarch, and salt in a medium saucepan. Gradually add the milk, stirring until the mixture is smooth. Bring the mixture to a boil over medium heat, stirring. Boil for 2 minutes. Remove the pan from the heat, stir some of the hot mixture into the egg yolks, then combine the egg yolk mixture with the rest of the mixture in the saucepan. Cook the custard over low heat, stirring, until it boils and thickens, about 5 minutes. Pour the custard into a bowl, and stir in half the coconut and the extracts. Cover the filling with waxed paper, and chill the filling for an hour. Pour the filling into the pie shell, and refrigerate the pie for 3 hours.

Just before serving, whip the cream, spread it over the filling, and top with the remaining coconut.

Yields 1 pie

Notes: To help keep the pie crust crisp, brush it with the egg whites before baking it, then let it cool before adding the filling.

To add extra flavor to the pie, add 6 inches of lemongrass stalk, 2 ounces ginger root, and a pinch of nutmeg to the milk mixture before heating it. Strain the mixture before combining it with the egg yolks.

If fresh coconut is not available, use 7 ounces flaked coconut that has been tossed with 1/4 teaspoon cinnamon and lightly toasted in the oven.

Baked Banana Custard

This easy-to-make, old-fashioned dessert is very welcome on a cold night.

4 ripe bananas
5 tablespoons sugar
1/2 teaspoon freshly grated nutmeg
Juice of 1 lime
1/2 cup dry, fine bread crumbs
3 eggs, beaten
2 cups hot milk

Preheat the oven to 350 degrees. Remove the threads from the bananas, and mash them. Add 2 tablespoons sugar, 1/4 teaspoon nutmeg, and the lime juice. Put the mashed bananas into a 10-inch oven-proof glass pie dish, and cover them with the bread crumbs.

Beat the rest of the sugar into the eggs until the sugar is dissolved. Slowly beat in the milk. Pour the egg-milk mixture over the mashed bananas in the glass dish. Sprinkle the remaining nutmeg on top. Bake the custard in a hot-water bath until it is set, about 45 minutes.

Serve hot or cold.

Yields 1 pie

Note: For extra flavor, try adding 1 ounce grated ginger and a vanilla bean to the milk while heating it (straining the milk before adding it to the beaten eggs).

Caramel Lime Sauce

This wonderful, clear caramel sauce goes with many desserts, especially flans, custards, and ice cream.

2 cups sugar
2 tablespoons water
1 1/2 cups heavy cream
1 cup lime juice

In a nonreactive pan, heat the sugar and water to a dark caramel. (Watch carefully and stir so you don't burn the sugar.) Remove the pan from the heat, stir in the cream, and then the lime juice.

Yields 2 to 2 1/2 cups

Rum Syrup

Try this syrup on pancakes, fritters, bread pudding, or anything else you can think of.

1 1/2 cups Jamaican light rum
2 1/2 cups sugar
1 1/2 cups warm strong tea
1/4 ounce gingerroot, sliced lengthwise
   into thin strips

In a saucepan, mix all the ingredients together until the sugar is dissolved. Bring the mixture to boil, and reduce it to 2 cups.

Strain out the ginger and discard it. Serve this syrup warm or cold.

Yields 2 cups

Note: Instead of discarding the ginger strips, you can roll them in sugar and bake them slowly to make a great ginger-rum candy.

Banana Fritters

Once you start making these, you may find that your family won't let you out of the kitchen. Proceed with caution!

4 very ripe bananas
1/4 coconut, finely grated
1/2 cup flour, sifted
1 1/2 teaspoons baking powder
2 1/2 tablespoons sugar
1 pinch freshly grated nutmeg
1/2 cup milk
1 teaspoon lemon juice
1 egg, beaten
Vegetable oil, for deep frying
Powdered sugar and cocoa powder, to
    dust the fritters

Purée the bananas to a cream. Fold the coconut into the bananas. In another bowl, mix together the flour, baking powder, sugar, and nutmeg. Stir the dry ingredients into the bananas and coconut, then the milk, egg, and lemon juice.

Drop the batter by tablespoons into 1/4-inch-deep hot oil. Drain the fritters on paper towels and sprinkle them with powdered sugar and cocoa powder.

Serve the fritters with hot honey or rum syrup.

Yields 12 to 16

Note: Several Jamaican banana varieties such as the lady's finger, the strawberry banana, and the apple banana (*manzano*), are smaller and much more delicately flavored than the common commercial banana and are often used for baked desserts. Try different varieties of bananas in this dish, if you can find them.

Sandra Forrester's Gizzadas

Everybody in Jamaica loves gizzadas or "pinch-me-rounds," as they are also called. Jay's grandmother ate them as a child on market days, his mom still craves them, and his adult brothers and sisters will still quarrel over who gets the last one.

Gizzadas are open-faced coconut tartlets with crimped edges. Sandra Forrester, the chef at the Bonnie View Hotel in Port Antonio, took the time to show Robb and Jay how to make them. She makes gizzadas at her home in batches of a hundred to sell to the local school-children. She always sells out before lunch break is over.

Tartlet Dough

8 cups flour
1/2 teaspoon salt
1/2 pound margarine, chilled
1/2 cup ice-cold water

Gizzada Filling

5 coconuts, grated, liquid reserved
1 cup water
2 pounds white or light brown sugar
1/4 pound ginger, peeled and grated
Pinch of nutmeg

To make the dough, sift the flour and the salt together. Cut the margarine into the flour until a coarse, crumbly meal is formed. Make a well, and add the cold water a little at a time, tossing with a fork until the water is absorbed. When the dough holds together with a pinch, enough water has been added. Shape the dough into a ball and knead it just till it is smooth. Wrap the dough, and place it in the refrigerator. Preheat the oven to 375 degrees.

"Cook the trash"—that is, cook the grated coconut with the water. When the coconut is almost dry, add the reserved coconut liquid, sugar, ginger, and pinch of nutmeg. Remove the pan from the heat.

Sandra Forrester makes gizzadas

Divide the chilled dough into 20 equal parts. On a lightly floured surface, roll out the dough to 1/8 inch thickness. Using a wide-mouthed drinking glass, cut out circles. To crimp the edges of the tart shells lift the dough up a little from the table and pinch with thumb and forefinger while pushing the dough just below with your other forefinger. The sides will be about 1/2 inch tall. Place the shells on ungreased baking sheets. Divide the coconut mixture among the shells. Bake until browned, about 20 minutes.

Remove the gizzadas from the baking sheets, and let them cool on wire racks. Serve warm.

Yields 100

Plantain Tarts

These are a lot like gizzadas, but they are made with plantain instead of coconut, and the filling is enclosed in the pastry. You don't have to color the filling red if you don't want to, but that's the tradition.

Tartlet Dough (see page 200)
3 very ripe, black plantains, peeled
1/2 cup sugar
1/2 teaspoon ground nutmeg
1/4 teaspoon vanilla extract
1/2 teaspoon almond extract
Pinch of salt
Drop of red food coloring
Sugar for garnish

Make the dough as for gizzadas (see page 200). Wrap and chill the dough.

In a pot, cover the plantains with water. Boil them until they are tender, about 15 minutes. Drain the plantains, and mash them until they are smooth. Blend in the sugar, nutmeg, almond and vanilla extracts, salt and red food coloring. Preheat the oven to 400 degrees.

Roll out the dough, and use a saucer or small plate to press out 8 circles, each 4 to 5 inches in diameter. Divide the plantain mixture into 8 parts, and place 1 part on half of each dough circle. Fold the other half over to form a half circle, then crimp the edges with a fork. Sprinkle the top with sugar, and bake the tarts on ungreased baking sheets for 30 to 45 minutes. Remove the tarts from the baking sheets, and let them cool on wire racks. Serve them hot or cold.

Serves 8

Note: If you hate to use red food coloring, steep a little sorrel (Jamaican hibiscus) in warm water, then use the water in boiling the plantains. You'll get the desired color without resorting to synthetics.

Cinnamon-Banana-Rum Mousse

Here's an elegant Jamaican dessert that combines some of Jamaica's most distinctive flavors. Save some of the cinnamon-flavored whipped cream for your coffee!

3/4 cup dark rum
2 tablespoons unflavored gelatin
3 ripe bananas, mashed
2 teaspoons vanilla extract
5 eggs, separated
Pinch of salt
1/3 cup superfine sugar
2 cups heavy cream
1 teaspoon ground cinnamon
1/8 teaspoon freshly grated nutmeg

Into a small nonreactive saucepan, pour 1/4 cup of the rum. Sprinkle the gelatin over the rum, and let the gelatin soak for a few minutes. Heat the rum and gelatin gently, while stirring, till the gelatin has completely dissolved. Remove the pan from the heat, and let the mixture cool.

Blend the bananas, the remaining 1/2 cup rum, and the vanilla to a smooth purée. Set the purée aside.

Beat the egg whites to stiff peaks. Add the salt and half the sugar gradually, beating constantly.

Beat the remaining sugar and pinch of salt with the egg yolks until the mixture is light and fluffy. Beat in 1 1/4 cups of the heavy cream. Keep beating until the cream is fully incorporated, about 5 minutes. Add the banana mixture to the cream mixture, then fold in the rum and gelatin. Gently fold in the egg whites. Pour the mixture into a lightly buttered glass mold, and refrigerate the mousse until set.

Beat the remaining cream with the cinnamon and nutmeg in a bowl till the cream is stiff. Pipe the cream decoratively on top of the mousse, and serve immediately.

Serves 6

Pioneer Chocolate Soufflé

Visiting the Pioneer Chocolate Factory in Williamsfield is like taking a walk in Willie Wonka's research and development lab. Tons of chocolate, cocoa butter, and powder are just waiting to be turned into dessert! This recipe does that fine Jamaican chocolate justice. Jay calls this soufflé the breakfast of champions, and he often has it with coffee in the morning.

3/4 pound unsalted butter
1 1/4 pounds bittersweet chocolate
1/2 pound milk chocolate
2 ounces Ortanique Liqueur (or Triple Sec)
3 tablespoons double-strength Blue Mountain Coffee
1 tablespoon ground cinnamon
1 tablespoon ground coriander
30 eggs, separated
2 cups sugar

Preheat the oven to 350 degrees. Butter and dust with flour two 4-inch-deep cake pans.

Melt the butter and chocolates with the liqueur, coffee, cinnamon and coriander in the top of a double boiler. Beat the mixture until it is smooth. Put the mixture into a large bowl. In another bowl, beat the egg yolks with the sugar. Fold the yolk-sugar mixture into the chocolate-butter mixture.

Beat the egg whites until stiff peaks form. Gently fold the egg whites into the chocolate mixture, being careful not to overwork them. Divide the batter between the two cake pans. Bake the soufflés for about an hour, or until the tops crack.

Remove the soufflés from the pans, and let them cool. (Jay likes this soufflé collapsed.) Serve them with a Caramel-Lime Sauce (page 198).

Serves 12 to 15

Notes: When separating the eggs, be sure that there are no yolks in the whites, or the whites won't fluff up to stiff peaks.

Try adding 1 cup chopped pecans or walnuts to the batter.

The recipe can be divided without any problems. (30 eggs is a lot!)

Coconut-Pimento Ice Cream

One of Jay's fondest memories of growing up in Jamaica is making ice cream with his grandfather. Even in his sixties, Grandpa would climb the coconut tree below his house to get three or four young coconuts—"jelly coconuts," as he called them—to make this coconut ice cream.

He had a wonderful old wooden hand-cranked ice cream bucket. He would pack the bucket with chipped ice and salt it down. Grandma would scald the milk and whip the eggs. When Grandma wasn't looking, Grandpa would always add his homemade pimento dram.

My brother and I would take turns cranking the bucket. It took what seemed like hours, and we always tired before the job was done, so Grandpa always had to finish it. That was the best ice cream in the world.

4 eggs, well beaten
1/2 cup sugar
2 cups whole milk, scalded, or 2 cups
    evaporated milk
1/2 teaspoon almond extract
1 teaspoon pimento dram
1 cup heavy cream
1 cup coconut jelly or coconut milk
1/2 cup fresh grated coconut
2 egg whites, beaten to stiff peaks

Combine the eggs and sugar, and beat them lightly. Stir in the scalded milk. In the top half of a double boiler, cook the mixture, stirring constantly with a wooden spoon, and paying particular attention to the edges, until the custard thickens and coats the spoon. When a line drawn across the back of the spoon holds, the custard is ready.

Place the top of the double boiler into an ice bath, and stir until the custard is cool. Stir in the almond extract and pimento dram. Mix the heavy cream, coconut jelly or milk, and coconut together, and add them to the ice cream base. Fold in the beaten egg whites.

Pour the ice-cream mixture into your ice-cream maker, and freeze it according to the manufacturer's instructions.

Serves 8

Banana-Caramel Ice Cream

Here's another favorite Jamaican flavor of ice cream.

3 ripe bananas, mashed (1 cup)
2 teaspoons lime juice
1/2 cup light brown sugar
1/4 teaspoon salt
1/3 cup milk
2 eggs, separated
1 cup heavy cream
1 teaspoon vanilla extract

In a bowl, mix the bananas and lime juice together. Stir in the sugar, salt and milk. Beat the egg whites until they are stiff. Beat the heavy cream until it is thick.

Beat the egg yolks until they are thick and creamy. Fold the egg whites into the banana mixture, fold in the egg yolks, and then the cream. The mixture should be thick and creamy. Stir in the vanilla last, then chill the mixture. After it is thoroughly chilled, put the bowl in the freezer, and stir the mixture every 20 to 30 minutes until it retains it shape, or freeze it in an ice-cream maker according to the manufacturer's instructions.

Serves 8

Stinking Toe (or Passion Fruit) Ice Cream

We promised to include stinking toe ice cream in this cookbook, and here it is!

30 egg yolks
2 eggs
4 cups sugar
1 gallon half-and-half
1/2 cup dark rum
2 cups stinking toe
    powder or passion
    fruit puree

Beat the yolks and eggs with the sugar. Heat the half-and-half to a simmer in a double boiler. Slowly beat the half-and-half into the yolks and sugar. Beat in the rum and stinking toe powder or passion fruit purée. Freeze in an ice-cream maker according to the manufacturer's instructions.

Yields 2 gallons ice cream

Easy Blue Mountain Coffee Ice Cream

3 cups double-strength Blue
  Mountain Coffee
1/4 cup sugar
1 cup marshmallow cream
2 cups heavy cream
1 cup half-and-half
1 teaspoon vanilla extract
1/4 teaspoon salt
Coffee Pecans (recipe follows)

Combine the coffee, sugar, and marshmallow cream in a saucepan. Cook the mixture over medium heat, stirring constantly, until it is well blended. Let the mixture cool, and then chill it.

Combine the coffee mixture, heavy cream, half-and-half, vanilla, and salt in a large mixing bowl, stirring until the ingredients are well blended. Pour the mixture into an ice-cream maker and freeze the ice cream according to the manufacturer's instructions. Let the flavors develop for 1 1/2 to 2 hours before serving (If you can!)

Scoop the ice cream into individual bowls, and garnish with coffee pecans.

Yields 1 gallon

Coffee Pecans

2 cups toasted pecan halves
1/4 cup sugar
2 teaspoons instant coffee granules
1/4 teaspoon ground pimento (allspice)
1/8 teaspoon salt
2 tablespoons water

Combine all the ingredients in a medium saucepan; mix them well. Bring the mixture to a boil. Boil it over medium heat for about 3 minutes, stirring constantly.

Spread the pecans on waxed paper, and separate them with a fork. Let them cool.

Yields 2 cups

Notes: Almonds and walnuts also work well in this recipe.

You can use 1/3 cup ginger syrup from Preserved Ginger (see page 159) instead of the sugar and water.

Blue Mountain Coffee Chiffon

Yes, there is such a thing as instant Blue Mountain coffee. Buy some while you're in Jamaica, and you'll be able to make this great dessert when you get home.

1 tablespoon powdered gelatin
3 tablespoons Instant Blue
    Mountain Coffee
1 cup water
2 cups milk
1 teaspoon vanilla extract
4 eggs, separated
3/4 cup sugar
1/4 cup fresh
    grated
    coconut, toasted

Dissolve the gelatin and coffee powder in the water over low heat. Stir in the milk and vanilla. Let the mixture stand in the refrigerator until it is almost set.

In the top part of a double boiler, beat the yolks and sugar until they are thick and creamy, remove the pan from the heat, then stir in the coffee mixture.

Beat the egg whites till they are very stiff. Gently fold them into the custard until the mixture is well blended (be careful not to overwork it). Pour the mixture into a glass serving bowl. Chill the chiffon for at least 4 hours.

Serve the chiffon sprinkled with the toasted coconut.

Serves 6

Plum Pudding

This is a very dense pudding, or "bun," that will help you to put on weight—so there'll be "more to love," as Grandma used to say.

3 cups sugar
1 pound unsalted butter, softened
10 eggs
1/2 cup coarse bread crumbs
1 cup flour, sifted
3 cups mixed dried or candied fruits
    (cherries, citron, ginger, pineapple),
    soaked 30 minutes in water
2 teaspoons cinnamon
1 teaspoon nutmeg
2 teaspoons pimento (allspice)
1 teaspoon cloves

1 tablespoon vanilla extract
1 tablespoon rum

Preheat the oven to 350 degrees.
    Cream together the butter and sugar. Beat in the eggs. Stir in the bread crumbs and flour. Fold in the fruits, spices, extract, and rum. Put the batter into a greased loaf pan, set in a pan of hot water. Bake for 2 to 2 1/2 hours, or until a toothpick inserted in the middle comes out clean.

Serves 6

Ackee Pudding

This is a very old Jamaican recipe.

2 cups milk
1/4 cup sugar
Grated nutmeg
3 cloves, ground
2 eggs, beaten
10 ackees, mashed fine

Preheat the oven to 350 degrees. Heat the milk with the sugar, a pinch of nutmeg, and the cloves until the mixture comes to a boil. Combine the milk with the eggs, and mix in the ackees. Pour the mixture into a buttered 9-inch pie dish, grate some nutmeg over the mixture, and bake until the pudding is set, about an hour. Serve the pudding hot.

Serves 2

Aunt Cassie's Pineapple Upside-Down Cake

Although this cake can be made in an hour and a half, Jay's Aunt Cassie used to take all day to make it. That was probably her way of adding all the love she could pour into it. She was always adamant about using the ripest pineapple, the best pecans, and the correct kind of flour. Everything was measured with scientific precision. The only time she ever had a problem in the twenty years she made this cake, she blamed it on Grandma's oven. "It's not calibrated correctly," she said.

1/2 cup unsalted butter
1 cup light brown sugar
2 pineapples, cored, then peeled, and
    sliced into rings (or 1 20-ounce can
    pineapple rings)
1/2 cup chopped pecans
10 maraschino cherries, halved
1 cup cake flour, sifted
1 teaspoon baking powder
1/4 teaspoon salt
4 eggs, at room temperature, separated
1 cup sugar
1 tablespoon melted unsalted butter
1 teaspoon almond extract

Preheat the oven to 325 degrees. In a 10-inch shallow ovenproof glass pie dish or heavy skillet, melt the 1/2 cup butter over low heat. Sprinkle the butter with the brown sugar. Arrange the pineapple rings in the bottom of the dish or skillet. Sprinkle the pecans and cherries around the pineapple slices.

Sift the flour with the baking powder and salt. Beat the egg whites until soft peaks form. Beat the egg yolks and sugar until they are very thick and yellow. Fold the flour mixture into the egg yolks. Gently fold the yolk-flour mixture into the egg whites until they are just combined (be careful not to overwork the batter). Fold in the 1 tablespoon butter and the almond extract.

Spread the batter evenly over the pineapple rings in the dish. Bake the cake for 30 to 35 minutes, or until the surface springs back gently when pressed. Loosen the edge of the cake, and let it stand on a wire rack for 10 minutes.

Invert the cake onto a serving plate, and serve it warm with vanilla ice cream.

Serves 8

Note: Jay often adds to the batter fresh ginger, guava marmalade, or both (2 to 3 teaspoons of each).

Mango Cheese

The mango tree was first introduced to Jamaica in 1782 from the East Indies. The ship carried several varieties of the fruit, and a great number of trees, so the trees were numbered according to the variety. Hence two of the more popular varieties have come to be known as Number 11 and Number 32. The Number 11 is a flat-sided green fruit, with a delicious aroma and acid taste. The Number 32 resembles the Number 11 in form and fragrance, but is yellow in color and possesses a more luscious sweetness. Use a Number 11 to make this great mango fudge known in Jamaica as "mango cheese."

12 Number 11 mangoes, peeled
3/4 cup sugar per cup of pulp
1/2 teaspoon lime juice per cup of pulp
1/2 inch of gingerroot per cup of pulp

Rub the mangoes through a sieve. Measure the pulp, and add the appropriate quantities of sugar and lime juice. In a nonreactive pan, bring the mixture to a boil. Add the ginger in big pieces so that they can be easily removed later. Boil the mixture, stirring continuously, until it is thick and leaves the side of the pan.

Remove the ginger and discard it. Pour the "cheese" onto a baking sheet that has a nonstick finish or has been rubbed with rum. The "cheese" should be about 1 inch thick. Let it cool. Cut the mango cheese to any size pieces you please and serve it.

Yields 2 pounds of "cheese"

Note: If you cut the ginger pieces into thin 1-inch squares after you remove them from the "cheese," you can roll them in sugar and bake them on a wire rack to make a great mango-ginger candy.

Coconut Drops

These little confections made with small bits of coconut in spiced brown sugar are a favorite with schoolchildren all over the island.

1/4 cup unsalted butter
1 cup brown sugar
2 eggs
1 teaspoon vanilla extract
1 cup milk
1 cup fresh grated coconut
1/2 cup coarsely chopped coconut
1/4 cup almond slivers or pecans
1/4 finely diced or grated gingerroot
1 cup flour
1/2 teaspoon baking powder
1/2 teaspoon ground cinnamon
1/8 teaspoon salt

Preheat the oven to 350 degrees. Lightly grease a baking sheet, and set it aside.

In a large bowl, blend the butter with the sugar until the mixture is creamy, then beat in the eggs, vanilla, and milk. Fold in the coconut, nuts, and ginger. Sift together the flour, baking powder, cinnamon, and salt. Add the dry ingredients to the coconut mixture, and blend well.

Drop about 2 tablespoons of the mixture at a time onto the prepared baking sheet. Bake the drops until they are golden brown, 15 to 20 minutes. Let them cool before serving.

Yields 30 drops

Stinking Toe Custard

Stinking toe looks like a big ugly toe with elephant-colored skin and smells like toe jam, if you can imagine that. Even more strange is that the powder inside the hard shell is eaten like candy by schoolchildren. Chances are you will never see a stinking toe, but, just in case you do, here is a recipe for you.

1/2 cup powder from 2 stinking toes
1 cup sugar
4 cups milk
1/8 teaspoon salt
8 eggs
1 teaspoon vanilla extract
6 tablespoons unsalted butter

Preheat the oven to 300 degrees.

Break the stinking toes in half, and shake out the powder. Mix the powder with the sugar. In a large saucepan, combine the milk and salt, and heat until bubbles form around the side of the pan. Remove the milk from the heat, add the sugar-stinking toe mixture, and stir until it is dissolved. In a large bowl, beat the eggs until they are fluffy, then gradually stir in the milk-stinking toe mixture. Add the vanilla, and stir well.

Melt the butter in a small skillet until it is golden, then pour the butter into a deep ovenproof glass quiche dish. Coat the bottom and sides of the dish with the butter. Pour the custard mixture into the dish. Place the pan in a shallow baking or roasting pan with water halfway up the sides of the quiche dish. Bake the custard for about an hour, or until a knife inserted in the center comes out clean.

Let the custard cool completely before inverting it onto a serving dish. Serve it with Rum Syrup (see page 198).

Serves 6

Jamaica's Fruits, Vegetables, and Spices

Jamaica is home to some of the world's most interesting fruits, vegetables and spices. Some are indigenous, but many favorite Jamaican staples are transplants. Breadfruit, for instance, was introduced by the infamous Captain Bligh on the H.M.S. Bounty. Legend has it that Captain Bligh's passionate regard for his breadfruit cuttings at the expense of the well-being of his crew led to the mutiny on the Bounty.

Here's a list of some of the fruits, vegetables and spices used in these Jamaican recipes:

Ackee
(also known as akee akee, and vegetable brain)
Brought to Jamaica from West Africa in the late 1700s, ackee is one of the strangest fruits in the world. It is poisonous if eaten underripe or overripe. For this reason ackee is forbidden to be imported into the United States. The edible portion has tiny brainlike fissures throughout. It has a mild vegetable flavor when cooked and resembles scrambled eggs in taste and appearance. Ackee and saltfish (salt cod) is a favorite Jamaican dish.

If you are unfamiliar with ackee, it is probably safest to use the canned variety.

Avocado
(also known as avocado pears)
Avocados are chiefly eaten at breakfast or lunch with pepper and salt. Sometimes they are eaten as a dessert, mashed with sugar, nutmeg, and rum.

Banana
In the 1960s, Panama disease wiped out huge numbers of Jamaican banana plantations. Many unique Jamaican varieties like the gros michel have all but disappeared since then. Now most plantations have been replanted with disease-resistant strains of the commercial banana. While Jamaica may not export many of its more exotic bananas anymore, they continue to be popular for cooking and eating on the island.

Plantains are very popular and so are green bananas which are eaten as a vegetable. For sweet recipes, apple bananas (manzanos) are a favorite. Other varieties of banana found in Jamaican markets include the gros michel, red bananas, and tiny lady fingers.

Barbados cherry
(also known as Syrian or Garden cherry)
A small, red, tart, indigenous berry that is very rich in vitamin C and is used in drinks and preserves.

Breadfruit
Breadfruit grows to a size a little larger than a softball. It has a green bumpy skin and is often roasted whole and then peeled. It is also made into pies and puddings. It has a bland, starchy flavor.

Byne spear, byne pear
These buds from flowering cactus plants are used like okra in the pepperpot soup made in the back country of St. Elizabeth.

Callaloo

The Jamaican green called callaloo tastes a lot like spinach and is used in much the same way. It's also very common in soups.

Cashew

Cashew nuts are familiar the world over, but Jamaicans also eat the fruit of the cashew. The cashew "apple" is sometimes stewed, and sometimes made into jelly or fermented for wine.

Cassava

(also known as manioc and tapioca)
Cassava was the staple of the indigenous Indians. There are two kinds of cassava, one which is "sweet" and the other poisonous when raw. Oddly, it is the poisonous cassava which is most commonly used. These cassava tubers are grated and then pressed to remove the poisonous prussic acid (cyanide), then the cassava is made into the flat loaves known as bammies.

Chewstick

Chewstick is the stem of a climbing vine which Jamaicans call a wiss. Cut pieces of the vine produce a foam that is used to add body to root beers and sodas. The foamy fibers of the chewstick are also used for brushing teeth, particularly by the Rastafarians.

Cho-cho squash

(also known as chayote and mirliton)
This very popular squash is common throughout Latin America. It looks like a large green pear, and it is usually served cooked, although it can be eaten raw.

Coconut

The recipes in this cookbook call for fresh coconut. If you use a canned substitute, read the label carefully since many products are sweetened and are not suitable for cooking.

To use a coconut, first pierce the eyes with an ice pick or a hammer and nail. Drain the liquid inside the coconut. This is coconut water.

Crack the shell with a hammer. Pry all of the coconut meat out of the broken shell with a blunt knife. Pare off the brown skin if you are making shredded coconut.

To make coconut milk, cut the meat into small pieces and grate in a food processor. Moisten with the coconut water and liquify. Pour boiling water on the liquified mixture and let it stand in a bowl for 30 minutes. Pass the mixture through a cheesecloth to separate the milk from the solids. Discard the solids. There are no firm rules regarding how much boiling water to use, but generally a whole coconut will yield as much as 8 cups of mild coconut milk or 4 cups of rich coconut milk.

Coffee

Jamaica's famous Blue Mountain coffee is considered by connoisseurs to be the finest in the world. Coffee is also used to flavor Tia Maria, the island's most popular liqueur.

Custard apple

A green, heart-shaped fruit with grape-like segments, the custard apple contains a very sweet white pulp with the consistency of pudding.

Dasheen

(Also known as coco and taro)
Dasheen tubers are the size of potatoes and are often compared in flavor to artichokes. They are cooked as vegetables and used to thicken stews and soups like mannish water. The coco is actually a closely related tuber that is slightly smaller in size.

Fever grass

Known as lemongrass in the Orient, fever grass is a stalky, weed-like grass that grows wild all over the island of Jamaica. It is used in Jamaica mainly for medicinal uses, hence the name.

Forbidden fruit
This is somewhat larger than a grapefruit. It is named for the three brownish marks on the peel, supposedly prints Eve made as she plucked the fruit. It is a hybrid of an orange and a shaddock (pomelo) and is very juicy.

Ginger
Jamaica is a large commercial producer and exporter of ginger. Both fresh and ground ginger are very common in Jamaican cooking. Jamaican ginger beer, a popular beverage, is much spicier than the ginger ale common in other parts of the world.

Grapefruit
Grapefruit originated in Jamaica, when a large, bitter, thick-skinned citrus fruit called shaddock or pomelo crossed with the sweet orange.

Guava
The guava was well known to the native Arawak Indians of Jamaica. A small yellow fruit when ripe, it is eaten raw, stewed, or as an excellent juice.

Guinep
(also known as honeyberry)
These little green fruits are sold in plastic bags in markets all over Jamaica. The pulp has a grape-like consistency and flavor. The large seeds, notorious for choking babies, can be roasted and eaten like chestnuts. The fruit was brought to Jamaica from Surinam.

Gungo peas
(also known as pigeon peas or no-eye peas)
The dish "rice and peas" is usually made with these small green peas, which are usually dried and split.

Irish moss
This white, stringy, edible seaweed found around the coast of Jamaica is reputed to have all sorts of health benefits. It is often used in making Jamaican tonics.

Jackfruit
Jackfruit is related to breadfruit, and the two are similar in appearance. Jackfruits reach enormous sizes, sometimes weighing 40 to 50 pounds. They are eaten both raw and cooked.

Jumblime
(also known as othaiti gooseberry)
This acidic berry, which people either love or hate, is very popular for preserves. The pale green, ribbed berries grow from both the branches and trunk of a tree.

June plum
Imported from the South Pacific, this sweet, pungent fruit has a fibrous seed and a bright yellow skin. June plums are highly prized when ripe and somewhat hard to find.

Mace
Mace is the lacy outer covering of the nutmeg kernel. It is pink when fresh and dries to a pale brown. It is used to flavor porridge and fruit drinks.

Mammee
Indigenous to the Caribbean, the mammee's apricot-colored fruit is usually eaten raw.

Mango
Ripe mangoes are popular in Jamaica as they are in many other parts of the world, but Jamaicans have come to know their mangos by the number. It seems that the ship that brought the mango to Jamaica brought a great many different varieties. To this day Jamaicans speak of Number 11s and Number 32s when they talk about mangos. The

numbers refer to different varieties among the numbered transplants that were brought to the island in 1782.

Naseberry

(also known as sapodilla)
The naseberry fruit grows on the tree that produces chicle, a gum used to make chewing gum. Naseberries are reddish brown outside with a translucent pulp that is sweet and fragrant. The Spanish thought this was the best fruit of the tropics.

Nutmeg

The peach-like fruit of the nutmeg tree contains a nut covered with a lacy scarlet skin. The nut is nutmeg, which is used ground or grated, as a spice. The red lacy covering is the spice known as mace.

Ortanique

The ortanique is a cross between the sweet orange and tangerine. The name comes from a combination of the words orange, tangerine, and unique. Like a tangerine, this sweet fruit has an easy-to-peel skin.

Othaiti apple

Brought to Jamaica in 1793 from Tahiti, this bright red, pear-shaped fruit has a white pulp and tastes like a cross between a pear and a coconut.

Passion fruit

Purple when ripe, the passion fruit has an orange pulp with black seeds. It has a very distinctive flavor, especially popular in drinks and ice cream.

Pawpaw

Pawpaw is the Jamaican name for papaya, a tropical fruit that is unrelated to the pawpaw native to the United States. Jamaican pawpaw flesh is more intensely colored and flavored than that of most other varieties of papaya. Pawpaw is very popular for breakfast.

Pimento

The Jamaican name for allspice is pimento. While cooks around the world are familiar with the dried berries, Jamaicans also use the leaves of the pimento tree in cooking. Pimento wood is highly prized for smoking jerked meats.

Pumpkin

(also known as Big Mama squash or calabacita). Jamaican pumpkins are green on the outside with orange flesh. Their flavor resembles that of winter squash.

Rose Apple

The flesh of the rose apple tastes like roses. The fruit is small and round, and yellow when ripe. An import form Malaysia, the rose apple grows wild in Jamaica.

Scotch bonnet peppers

A member of the capsicum chinense family, the Scotch bonnet is among the hottest peppers in the world. It is related to the habanero of Mexico and the datil pepper of Florida. The Scotch bonnet is named for the distinctive shape of the fruit; it has a wavy ridge around the middle which makes it look a little like a tufted cap. It is found in Jamaican markets in colors ranging from green to orange to bright red. Despite its extreme heat, the Scotch bonnet has a pleasant fruity taste.

Sea grapes

These tart fruits with large seeds hang in clusters from trees that grow wild near the beach. Jamaicans munch on the the ripe fruits where they grow, but seldom use them in cooking.

Shaddock

Shaddock is a citrus fruit that originated in

Polynesia. It was brought to the West Indies by an English sea captain named Shaddock, who gave the fruit its name. It is a somewhat bitter fruit with a thick skin, so it's not very popular. But its introduction to Jamaica was very fortunate anyway—through crossbreeding, genetic mutation, or both the shaddock eventually gave birth to a new citrus fruit, the grapefruit.

Soursop

Native to the American tropics, the soursop is a heart-shaped fruit with a green, spiky skin. The white custardy interior is very aromatic and very popular in drinks and desserts.

Star apple

The star apple is purple when it is ripe. If you cut one in half, you see the star pattern that gave the fruit its name. The star apple is mild and sweet and most often eaten in a fruit salad with oranges.

Stinking toe

This bizarre "fruit" is actually a pod that looks like a human toe. The rough exterior smells awful, but inside is a sugary powder that kids eat on the spot and some people use to make custard.

Sugarcane

Sugarcane plantations were once the dominant force in Jamaica's economy. Sugar, molasses, vinegar, and rum are all produced from this overgrown member of the grass family. It takes ten tons of sugarcane to make one barrel of rum!

Susumber

(also known as gully bean or turkeyberry)
This very common wild berry is a little smaller than a cherry and looks like an oversized caper. It has a sour, bitter flavor and is often eaten as a condiment with saltfish.

Sweetsop

The sweetsop fruit is smaller than the soursop and has a rough green skin without spikes. The sweet pulp surrounds a multitude of black seeds.

Tamarind

The small brown pods have an aromatic pulpy interior with large seeds. The pulp is used in sauces, beverages, and sweets including such well-known products as Angostura bitters and Pickapeppa Sauce.

Ugli fruit

(also known as hoogly)
A cross between an orange and a grapefruit, hoogly looks weird and misshapen, but it's very sweet eating.

Yam

The yam has been a staple food of Jamaica since prehistoric times. There are several varieties of Jamaican yams. The Negro yam is large with black skin and a white-yellow flesh. The Indian yam or yampee is sweet, and the somewhat rare arracacha yam tastes a little like parsnips. But the yellow yam is by far the most popular. It is also generally the largest, growing to sizes in excess of fifteen pounds.

Sources of Caribbean Foods and Information

Midwest

Peppery Palate
4500 16th St.
South Park Mall
Moline, IL 61265

North East

Brooklyn Terminal Market
Liberty Ave.
Brooklyn, NY 11207

Caribbean Heat
1915 Ulysses St.
Minneapolis, MN 55418

**Casa Hispania International
Food Market**
PO Box 587
73 Poningo St.
Port Chester, NY 10578
(914) 939-9333

Dean & Deluca
560 Broadway, Suite 304
New York, NY 10012
(800) 221-7714 (except NY)
(800) 431-1691 (NY)
Imported and domestic specialty foods.

Island Cooking Kitchens
1245 Park Ave.
New York, NY 10028
(212) 860-8810
Jerk marinades. Contact:
Dunstan Harris

Jamaica Tourist Board
866 Second Ave., 10th floor
New York, NY 10017
(212) 688-7650
In Jamaica, (809) 929-9200

**Jampro (Jamaican Commerce
Promotion and Information)**
866 2nd Ave., 6th floor
New York, NY 10017
(212) 371-4800

**Pepper's/Starboard
Restaurant**
2009 Highway One at
Saulsbury St.
Dewey Beach, DE

Pica Gourmet
11864 Sunrise Valley Dr.
Reston, VA 22091

Port Royal Foods, Inc.
P.O. Box 881
Hicksville, NY 11802
Contact: Irving Zwecker

South

Blue Mountain Imports, Inc.
7022 N.W. 50th St.
Miami, FL 33166
(305) 594-9244
Caribbean sauces and marmalades. For retail outlets.

Creole Delicacies
#1 Poydras St.
New Orleans, LA 70130

Caribbean Spice Co.
2 South Church
Fairhope, AL 36532

Dekalb World Farmers Market
3000 E. Ponce de Leon
Decatur, GA 30034
(404) 377-6401

Dewars Fine Foods
1937 Peachtree Road
Atlanta, GA 30309
(404) 351-3663

Goya
1900 N.W. 92nd Ave.
Miami, FL 33172
(305) 592-3150

Harry's Farmers Market
1180 Upper Hembree Rd.
Alpharetta, GA
(404) 664-6300

Helen's Tropical-Exotics
3519 Church St.
Clarkston, GA 30021
GA: (404) 292-7278
Wholesalers and retailers:
(800) 544-JERK
Seasonings, marinades, sauces.

Jamaica Groceries & Spices
9628 S.W. 160th St.
Colonial Shopping Centre
Miami, FL 33157
(305) 252-1197

J.R. Brooks and Son, Inc.
P.O. Drawer 9
18400 SW 256th St.
Homestead, FL 33090-0009
(800) 423-4808 (FL)
(800) 327-4833 (outside FL)
(800) 338-1022 (Canada)
Tropical fruits.

Kingston-Miami Trading Co.
280 N.E. 2nd St.
Miami, FL 33132
(305) 372-9547

La Preferida, Inc. (Florida)
9108 N.W. 105th Way
Medley, FL 33178
(305) 883-8444
Contact: Carlos Bordon

West Indian Food Specialties
6035 Miramar Parkway
Miramar, FL 33023
(305) 962-6418

West

Anjos Imports
P.O. Box 4031
Cerritos, CA 90703-4031
(310) 865-9544
Jamaican Condiments & spices

Bay Cities Imports
1517 Lincoln Blvd.
Santa Monica, CA 90401

Consentino's Market
2666 S. Bascom Ave.
San Jose, CA 95124

Farmers Market
6333 Third St.
Los Angeles, CA 90036

Frieda's Finest Produce Specialties
P.O. Box 58488
Los Angeles, CA 90058
(213) 627-2981 (CA)
(800) 421-2981 (outside CA)
Exotic fruits and vegetables.
Mail order.

Horton Farmers Market
One Horton Plaza
San Diego, CA 92101

Hots For You
6919 S. Highland Dr.
Salt Lake City, UT 84121

International Market
2020 Parker Rd.
Denver, CO 80231

Jones & Bones
621 Capitola Ave.
Capitola, CA 95010
(408) 462-0521
Caribbean condiments, sauces, and spices. Mail order.

La Preferida, Inc. (Texas)
4000 Telephone Rd.
Houston, TX 77087
(713) 643-7128
Contact: Edgar Martinez

Larry's Market
10008 Aurora Ave. N.
Seattle, WA 98133

Rainbow Grocery
1899 Mission St.
San Francisco, CA 94103

Some Like It Hot
3208 Scott St.
San Francisco, CA 94123

Canada

Toronto Caribbean Corner
57 Kensington Ave.
Toronto, Ont.
(416) 593-0008

Tropical Harvest Food Market
57 Kensington Ave.
Toronto, Ont.
(416) 593-9279

West Indian Fine Foods
Terrace Brae Plaza
Markham & Lawrence
Scarborough, Ont.
(416) 431-9353

Index

***The
Crossing Press***

*publishes a full selection
of cookbooks. To receive
our current catalog, please
call, toll-free,
800 / 777-1048.*